# ON COURSE 1

# ON COURSE 1
**student book**

**Carol Cellman**
Oxford University Press · 1988

Oxford University Press

200 Madison Avenue
New York, NY 10016 USA

Walton Street
Oxford OX2 6DP England

OXFORD is a trademark of Oxford University Press.

**Library of Congress Cataloging-in-Publication Data**

Cellman, Carol
  On Course. Student Book 1.

  1. English language—Textbooks for foreign speakers.  I. Title.
[PE1128.C4457  1988      428.2′4      88-12547
ISBN 0-19-434285-9
ISBN 0-19-434286-7 (Teacher's book 1)
ISBN 0-19-434287-5 (Cassette, 1)

Copyright © 1988 Oxford University Press.

All rights reserved. No part of this publication may be reproduced, stored in a retrieval system, or transmitted, in any form or by any means, electronic, mechanical, photocopying, recording, or otherwise, without the prior permission of Oxford University Press.

This book is sold subject to the condition that it shall not, by way of trade or otherwise, be lent, resold, hired out, or otherwise circulated without the publisher's prior consent in any form of binding or cover other than that in which it is published and without a similar condition including this condition being imposed on the subsequent purchaser.

Cover Design by Mark Kellogg
"Breck Marshall" photograph by Nancy d'Estang. All rights reserved, the Mystic Seaport Museum, Inc.

Illustrators:
Kathie Abrams, Lisa Adams, Michael Bartalos, Rick Brown, Yvonne Buchanan, David Cain, Kevin Callahan, David Celsi, Tennessee Dixon, Tom Graham, Laura Hartman Maestro, Steve Marchesi, Shelley Matheis, Mark Rowney, Arnie Ten, and Anna Veltfort

Photography:
Richard Haynes, Jr. and Cynthia Hill

Styling and locations:
Nancy Haffner

The publisher would like to thank the following for permission to reproduce photographs:
Mark Antman/The Image Works; Focus On Sports; Dan Helms/Duomo Photography, Inc.; Japan National Tourist Organization; Dee Quinones & Patrick Taverna/American Ballroom Theatre Co.; Ebet Roberts; Raymond Ross; Steven Speliotis/American Ballroom Theatre; Susanne Faulkner Stevens/New York Philharmonic; Adam Stoltman/Duomo Photography, Inc.; and Martha Swope.

Graphics:
Terry Helms and April Okano

Developmental Editor: Debbie Sistino
Associate Editor: Lisa Ahlquist
Design Manager: Shireen Nathoo
Senior Designer: Mark Kellogg
Art Researcher: Paula Radding

Printing (last digit): 9 8 7 6 5 4 3 2 1

Printed in Hong Kong

# Preface

*On Course* is an easy-to-use, two-level speaking and listening course for young adults and adults who are beginning their study of English. Full-color, humorous illustrations and photographs support grammar and new vocabulary.

Both Books 1 and 2 follow a carefully sequenced grammatical syllabus and integrate communicative functions throughout. Topics include introductions, occupations, pastimes, shopping, transportation, restaurants, and everyday living.

The books are divided into 30 two-page units. Lessons have been developed so that they can be accomplished in 50-minute periods. Pair practice and information gap exercises provide many opportunities for student interaction. The six four-page summary units naturally recombine and reinforce the material that has been presented throughout the 30 units. A task listening activity is a regular feature of each summary unit.

The accompanying Teacher's Books are interleaved and include suggestions for presenting each lesson, a detailed syllabus, a word list, and a tapescript.

The Cassettes contain all of the dialogues and task listening sections in the Student Books.

# Table of Contents

| Unit | | Page |
|---|---|---|
| 1 | This is my family. | 2 |
| 2 | Say the numbers. | 4 |
| 3 | Please send a taxi right away. | 6 |
| 4 | Who's that over there? | 8 |
| 5 | What time's the concert? | 10 |
| Summary 1 | Units 1–5 | 12 |
| 6 | But they're expensive . . . | 16 |
| 7 | Are you all right? | 18 |
| 8 | What's the matter? | 20 |
| 9 | What's in the living room? | 22 |
| 10 | Oh, yes—room 307 is excellent! | 24 |
| Summary 2 | Units 6–10 | 26 |
| 11 | By the way, how much is it? | 30 |
| 12 | Go one block to Maple Avenue. | 32 |
| 13 | What's happening? | 34 |
| 14 | Is she going to classes this week? | 36 |
| 15 | Don't forget your keys! | 38 |
| Summary 3 | Units 11–15 | 40 |
| 16 | Do you need a racket? | 44 |
| 17 | Do you like baseball? | 46 |
| 18 | Are you ready to order? | 48 |
| 19 | Is that one-way or round-trip? | 50 |
| 20 | I don't feel well today. | 52 |
| 21 | I usually get up at 7:30. | 54 |
| Summary 4 | Units 16–21 | 56 |
| 22 | This restaurant was great last year. | 60 |
| 23 | A week ago, we were in Florida . . . | 62 |
| 24 | I called all day. | 64 |
| 25 | How was the party? | 66 |
| 26 | When I was 17, I broke my arm. | 68 |
| Summary 5 | Units 22–26 | 70 |
| 27 | Please, can you help me? | 74 |
| 28 | How many do you need? | 76 |
| 29 | It's the nicest restaurant around. | 78 |
| 30 | I'm going to need your help. | 80 |
| Summary 6 | Units 27–30 | 82 |
| Word and phrase list | | 86 |

Unit 1   This is my family.

**1  Listen to the conversation and practice with a partner.**

BEN:   Tom, this is my family.
TOM:   Who's that?
BEN:   That's my (1.) *wife*.

**Have similar conversations with a partner.**

2. mother        3. son          4. brother       5. father
6. aunt          7. sister       8. daughter      9. grandfather

**2  Listen to the conversation and practice with a partner.**

TOM:   Is that your *wife?*
BEN:   No, my *wife's* very *short*.

**Have similar conversations with a partner. Use words from the box.**

1. mother        2. son          3. brother
   tall             young

4. father        5. aunt         6. sister
                                    Yes, it is!

tall
short
old
young

2

## 3 Listen to the conversation and practice with partners.

BEN: Tom, this is my *sister, Janet*. *She's* from *L.A.*
TOM: It's nice to meet you, *Janet*.
JANET: Nice to meet you, too.

BEN: Tom, this is my *grandfather, Mr. Stone*. *He's* from *New York*.
TOM: How do you do, *Mr. Stone*?
MR. STONE: How do you do, Tom?

**Introduce Tom to these people. Choose the first conversation or the second conversation.**

1. brother/Mark
   Boston
2. aunt/Christine
   Denver
3. wife/Maria
   Puerto Rico
4. mother and father
   Mr. and Mrs. Miller
   Chicago

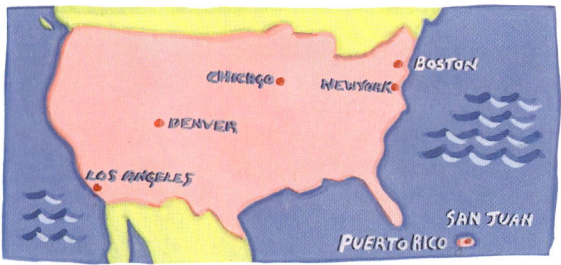

## 4 Introduce your partner to three other students in your class.

A: _____(Student B)_____, this is _____(Student C)_____.
   She's/He's from _____(city)_____.
B: It's nice to meet you, _____(Student C)_____.
C: Nice to meet you, too.

| GRAMMAR | | | | | USEFUL LANGUAGE |
|---|---|---|---|---|---|
| Who's | that? | | Yes, | it is. | It's nice to meet you. |
| Is | that | your wife? | No, | my wife's very short. | Nice to meet you, too. |
| | That's | my wife. | | | How do you do? |
| This is | Janet. | | She's | from L.A. | |
| | Mr. Stone. | | He's | | |

Unit 2  Say the numbers.

# 1

**Listen to the numbers.**

| 1  | 2  | 3  | 4  | 5  | 6  | 7   | 8  | 9  | 10 | 11 | 12 | 13 |
|----|----|----|----|----|----|-----|----|----|----|----|----|----|
| 14 | 15 | 16 | 17 | 18 | 19 | 20  | 21 | 22 | 23 | 24 | 25 | 26 |
| 27 | 28 | 29 | 30 | 31 | 32 | 33  | 34 | 35 | 36 | 37 | 38 | 39 |
| 40 | 50 | 60 | 70 | 80 | 90 | 100 | •  | •  | •  | •  | •  | •  |

**Listen again and repeat.**

**Listen to the letters.**

| Aa | Bb | Cc | Dd | Ee | Ff | Gg | Hh | Ii | Jj |
|----|----|----|----|----|----|----|----|----|----|
| Kk | Ll | Mm | Nn | Oo | Pp | Qq | Rr | Ss |    |
| Tt | Uu | Vv | Ww | Xx | Yy | Zz | •  | •  | •  |

**Listen again and repeat.**

# 2

**Listen to the game and play it with a partner.**

A: Write four numbers, please.
B: OK. Don't look.

A: Now tell me the numbers.
B: *9 6 1 3.*

A: Tell me the numbers again.
B: *9 6 1 3.* Now you say the numbers.
A: *9 6 1 3.* Is that right?

B: Yes/No, it's ____ ____ ____ ____. Now write the numbers.
A: (writes) Is this right?
B: Yes/No.

A: Now you ask me.
B: OK. Write four numbers, please.

**Now play the game with letters.**

# 3

**Listen to the conversation and practice with a partner.**

A: Say the number before *7.*
B: *6.*
A: Say the number after *7.*
B: *8.*

**Ask and answer questions like these about numbers and letters with a partner.**

Say the number before ____.
Say the number after ____.
Say the letter before ____.
Say the letter after ____.

## 4

**Listen to the conversation and practice with partners.**

MARIA: Hi, Anna.
ANNA: How are you, Maria?
MARIA: I'm fine. And you?
ANNA: I'm OK.
TEACHER: Please sit down now. It's time for class.
MARIA: See you after class, OK?
ANNA: OK.

## 5

**Listen to the conversations and practice with partners.**

TEACHER: Open your books to page 3, please.
STUDENT A: Please repeat that.
TEACHER: Open your books to page 3.
STUDENT A: Thank you.

TEACHER: Now look at the picture. Listen to the conversation on the tape. Don't repeat.
TAPE: This is my sister, Janet. She's from L.A.

TEACHER: Now repeat the conversation.
TAPE: This is my sister, Janet. She's from L.A.
STUDENTS: This is my sister, Janet. She's from L.A.

TEACHER: Now practice the conversation with a partner.
STUDENT A: This is my sister, Janet. She's from L.A.
STUDENT B: It's nice to meet you, Janet.
STUDENT A: Nice to meet you, too.

STUDENT A: What does "L.A." mean?
TEACHER: "L.A." means Los Angeles.

| GRAMMAR | | | | USEFUL LANGUAGE | |
|---|---|---|---|---|---|
| Is | this | right? | Don't repeat. | Hi, _____. | Please repeat that. |
| | that | | Repeat. | How are you? | Thank you. |
| | | | | I'm fine. | What does L.A. mean? |
| | | | | OK. | L.A. means Los Angeles. |
| | | | | And you? | |

Unit 3  Please send a taxi right away.

## 1

**Listen to the conversation and practice with a partner.**

OPERATOR: Hello?
SAM MASON: Hello. Is this the ABC Taxi Company?
OPERATOR: Yes.
SAM: Please send a taxi right away.
OPERATOR: OK. What's your name?
SAM: *Sam Mason.*
OPERATOR: Please spell it.
SAM: *M-A-S-O-N.*
OPERATOR: And what's your address?
SAM: *32 Long Street.*
OPERATOR: Uh-huh. Now what's your phone number?
SAM: *565-7953.*

**Have similar conversations with a partner.**

1. Jack Simms
   124 River Street
   323-4956

2. Anna Fine
   107 Green Street
   789-3362

3. Ted Newman
   915 King Avenue
   956-2258

4. Bob Marshall
   809 Johnson Street
   682-0748

5. Kate Baker
   716 Central Avenue
   373-8925

6. Tina Moss
   411 Main Street
   977-4155

## 2

**Listen to the conversation and practice with a partner.**

DRIVER: Taxi for *Sam Mason.*
MAN: Who?
DRIVER: *Sam Mason. M-A-S-O-N.* Is *he* here?
MAN: No. What's *his* address?
DRIVER: *32 Long Street.*
MAN: Oh. *32 Long Street* is over there.
DRIVER: Thank you very much!
MAN: You're welcome.

**Have similar conversations about the people in Part 1.**

## 3

**Ask three students in your class these questions.**

What's your name? Please spell it.
What's your address?
What's your phone number?

**Check your answers.**

Is your name _____? address _____? phone number _____?

## 4

**Listen to the conversation and practice with a partner.**

DRIVER: Is she your daughter?
SAM: Yes.
DRIVER: How old is she?
SAM: She's eight.

## 5

**Ask three students in your class these questions and write the answers.**

A: How old is your *sister?*
B: *She's 8.* (or) I don't have a *sister.*
A: How old is your _____?

| Name | Sister | Brother | Father |
|---|---|---|---|
| Student 1 | | | |
| Student 2 | | | |
| Student 3 | | | |

GRAMMAR

| What's | your<br>his<br>her | name?<br>address?<br>telephone number? |

| Is your | name<br>address<br>telephone number | _____ ? |

| Is she | your daughter?<br>here?<br>over there? |

| How old is | she?<br>your brother? |

| She's<br>He's | eight. |

| I don't have | a sister.<br>a brother. |

USEFUL LANGUAGE

Hello.
Is this the ABC Taxi Company?
Please send a taxi.
Please spell it.
Thank you very much.
You're welcome.

7

Unit 4 Who's that over there?

**1** **Listen to the conversation and practice with a partner.**

ALICIA: That's my neighbor. *He's* very nice.
MOTHER: Where's *he* from?
ALICIA: *He's* from *Spain,* I think.
MOTHER: Is *he* married?
ALICIA: No, *he's single.*
MOTHER: Is *he* a student?
ALICIA: No, *he's an artist.*

Use *an* before words that begin with A, E, I, O, or U.
He's *an a*rtist.
She's *an E*nglish teacher.

**Have similar conversations with a partner.**

1. France
   divorced
   factory worker

2. Vietnam
   single
   accountant

3. the United States
   married
   secretary

4. Japan
   married
   nurse

5. Brazil
   divorced
   businesswoman

6. China
   single
   taxi driver

7. Greece
   divorced
   engineer

8. the Philippines
   married
   waitress

## 2

**Listen to the conversation and practice with a partner.**

MOTHER: Alicia, who's that over there?
ALICIA: The *short woman* with *dark* hair?
MOTHER: Yes.
ALICIA: That's my friend, *Lisa*. She's a *lawyer*.
MOTHER: Oh? Where's *she* from?
ALICIA: *She's* from *Italy*.
MOTHER: Really? Is *she* married?
ALICIA: No, *she's single*.
MOTHER: Excuse me?
ALICIA: *She's single*.
MOTHER: Oh.

**Have similar conversations with a partner.**

1. short woman/dark
   Sasha/cook
   Russia
   single

2. tall man/dark
   David/doctor
   the United States
   divorced

3. tall man/dark
   Kenji/businessman
   Japan
   single

4. short woman/blond
   Ute/student
   Germany
   single

5. short man/dark
   Park/waiter
   Korea
   divorced

6. tall woman/blond
   Sheila/English teacher
   Canada
   divorced

## 3

**Work with a partner. Tell about a friend or relative. Use the conversation in Part 2.**

| GRAMMAR | | | | | | | USEFUL LANGUAGE |
|---|---|---|---|---|---|---|---|
| Is he | a student? married? | | | He's She's | single. an artist. very nice. | | . . . I think. Really? Excuse me? Oh. |
| Where's | he she | from? | | He's She's | from | Spain. the United States. | |
| a | doctor | | | | | | |
| an | artist | | | | | | |

Unit 5   What time's the concert?

## 1  Listen and say the days of the week.

## 2  Listen and say these times.

eight o'clock    eight-fifteen    eight-thirty    eight forty-five
                 or                               or
                 a quarter after eight            a quarter to nine

**Now practice with a partner. Start like this:**

A:   What time is it?
B:   It's _____.

## 3  Listen to the conversation and practice with a partner.

A: When's the concert?
B: 7:00.
A: What time is it now?

B: It's 6:15.
A: Oh, I'm early.
B: Yes. Please wait here.

B: It's 7:15.
A: Oh, I'm late.
B: Yes. Please go in quietly.

B: It's exactly 7:00.
A: Oh, I'm on time.
B: Yes. Please go in.

**Practice with these times.**

1. 6:30   2. 7:30   3. 6:00   4. 8:00   5. 7:45

## 4

**Listen to the conversation and practice with a partner.**

A: What time's the concert?
B: 7:00.
A: Oh, I'm on time.
B: No, you're early.
A: Early? It's *exactly 7:00.*
B: The concert is Wednesday. Today's Tuesday.
A: Oh, no!

## 5

**Listen to the conversation and practice with a partner.**

A: Look at that *tall woman—she's* famous!
B: Famous? Are you sure?
A: Yes, that's *Linda Landon. She's* on TV.
B: What program?
A: The *News Hour.* It's on *Friday* at *10:30.*
B: A.M. or P.M.?
A: *P.M.*
B: Oh, now I remember.

**Have similar conversations with a partner. Student A, look on the left.
Tell Student B about two famous people. Student B, look on the right.
Tell Student A about two famous people.**

### STUDENT A

1. blond man
Harry Horner
Music Hour
Saturday/9:00 / A.M.

2. blond woman
Susan Shaw
Cooking Hour
Sunday/10:00 /A.M.

### STUDENT B

3. short woman
Carol Carson
Comedy Hour
Thursday/8:00 /P.M.

4. heavy man
Bob Bigby
Sports Hour
Wednesday/8:30 /P.M.

| GRAMMAR | | | | | USEFUL LANGUAGE |
|---|---|---|---|---|---|
| When's<br>What time's | the concert? | | I'm<br>You're | early.<br>late.<br>on time. | What time is it?<br>It's (exactly) _____.<br>Please wait here.<br>Please go in quietly. |
| Today's<br>It's<br>On | Monday. | | At 10:30 A.M. | | Oh, no!<br>Are you sure?<br>When's it on?<br>A.M or P.M.?<br>Oh, now I remember. |

Summary 1  Units 1–5

## 1
**Listen and circle the letter of the best answer.**

a. Thank you.
(b.) B-O-B.

1. a. Good-bye.
   b. Nice to meet you.

2. a. Wednesday at 2:00.
   b. About 25.

3. a. Tuesday.
   b. Thursday.

4. a. You're welcome.
   b. Excuse me.

5. a. Mexico.
   b. Over there to the right.

6. a. 3:00.
   b. Thursday.

7. a. Oh—I'm late!
   b. You're welcome.

8. a. 491-0488.
   b. 119 Broad Street.

9. a. Fine. And you?
   b. Thank you.

10. a. No, he's a musician.
    b. Yes, she's divorced.

11. a. She's 27.
    b. He's 19.

12. a. She's from Puerto Rico.
    b. No, she's married.

## 2
**You are at a party. You don't know the people. Listen to these conversations. Write the information about three people. Choose from these words:**

| | | |
|---|---|---|
| Japan | student | divorced |
| the U.S. | engineer | single |
| Greece | nurse | married |
| Germany | artist | |
| Brazil | taxi driver | |

## 3
**Fill in the missing information in these messages from a phone answering machine.**

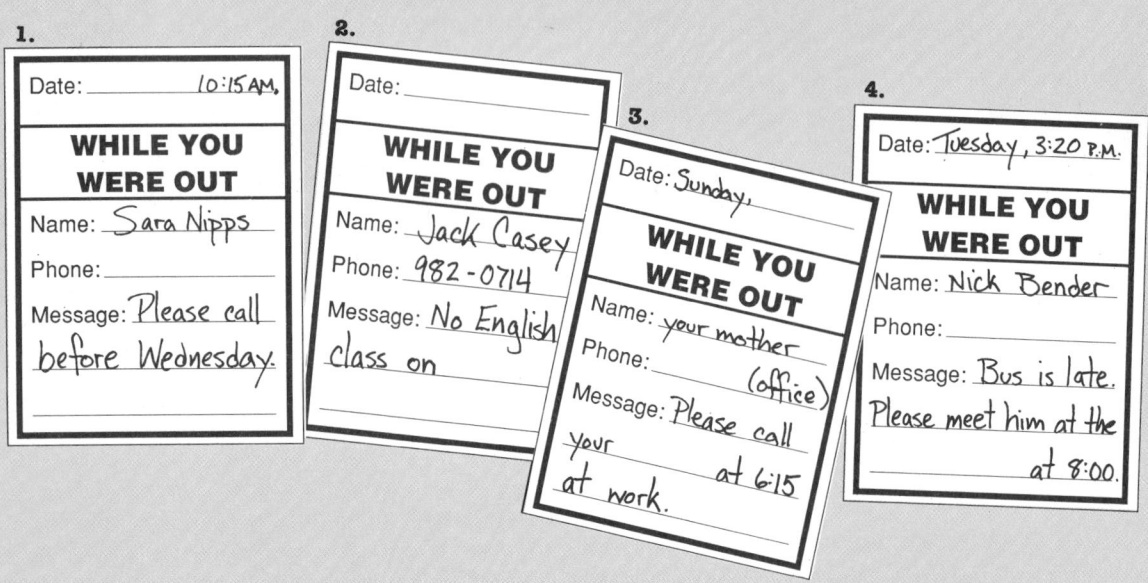

1. Date: 10:15 AM
   WHILE YOU WERE OUT
   Name: Sara Nipps
   Phone: ___
   Message: Please call before Wednesday.

2. Date: ___
   WHILE YOU WERE OUT
   Name: Jack Casey
   Phone: 982-0714
   Message: No English class on ___

3. Date: Sunday
   WHILE YOU WERE OUT
   Name: your mother
   Phone: ___ (office)
   Message: Please call your ___ at 6:15 at work.

4. Date: Tuesday, 3:20 P.M.
   WHILE YOU WERE OUT
   Name: Nick Bender
   Phone: ___
   Message: Bus is late. Please meet him at the ___ at 8:00.

Work with a partner for Parts 4 and 5. Student A, look at this page. Student B, look at the next page.

# STUDENT A

## 4

**What's the Message?**
Ask and answer questions with your partner.
Write the missing letters.

A: What letter is *1?*
B: *W.*

| | | | |
|---|---|---|---|
| 1 = W | 8 = Y | 15 = G | 22 = ___ |
| 2 = ___ | 9 = A | 16 = ___ | 23 = F |
| 3 = H | 10 = ___ | 17 = ___ | 24 = ___ |
| 4 = ___ | 11 = J | 18 = V | 25 = ___ |
| 5 = Q | 12 = ___ | 19 = ___ | 26 = L |
| 6 = ___ | 13 = X | 20 = I | |
| 7 = ___ | 14 = ___ | 21 = P | |

Work with your partner to write this message:

8   17   22   14   7   4   15   26   20   25   3   20   25

___ ___ ___ ___ ___ ___ ___ ___ ___ ___ ___ ___ ___

18   7   14   8   15   17   17   10

___ ___ ___ ___ ___ ___ ___ ___ .

## 5

Student A, start the conversation. Then listen to your partner and choose a good answer. Continue the conversation. Then try the conversation again. Choose different answers.

—Hi, Max! Say, how's your sister, Nina?

—A doctor? Where?
—Really? What's her phone number there?

—Is that in Mexico?
—Excuse me? Did you say 2–1–3?

—Santa Fe? Spell it, please.
—Is Nina married now?

—Thanks. Oh, no! I'm late for class. Please say hello to Nina, OK? Good-bye, Max.
—That's nice! Well, it's good to see you, Max.

13

# STUDENT B

## 4

**What's the Message?**
Ask and answer questions with your partner. Write the missing letters.

A: What letter is *1?*
B: *W.*

| | | | |
|---|---|---|---|
| 1 = W | 8 = ___ | 15 = ___ | 22 = U |
| 2 = C | 9 = ___ | 16 = Z | 23 = ___ |
| 3 = ___ | 10 = D | 17 = O | 24 = M |
| 4 = N | 11 = ___ | 18 = ___ | 25 = S |
| 5 = ___ | 12 = T | 19 = B | 26 = ___ |
| 6 = K | 13 = ___ | 20 = ___ | |
| 7 = E | 14 = R | 21 = ___ | |

**Work with your partner to write this message:**

8  17  22  14  7  4  15  26  20  25  3  20  25
___ ___ ___ ___ ___ ___ ___ ___ ___ ___ ___ ___ ___

18  7  14  8  15  17  17  10
___ ___ ___ ___ ___ ___ ___ ___ .

## 5

**Student B, listen to your partner and then choose a good answer. Continue the conversation. Then try the conversation again. Choose different answers.**

—She's fine. She's a doctor now.
—Just fine. She's in Los Angeles now.

—(213) 555-4330.
—In New Mexico.

—Yes, (213) 555-4330.
—No, it's in the U.S. She's in Santa Fe.

—S-A-N-T-A  F-E.
—Yes, Her husband is from Hong Kong.

—OK. Good-bye, Cindy.
—It's nice to see you, too.

14

## 6 Game

1. Write a number from 0 to 10 to the left of E and another number to the right of E.
2. Write a number from 11 to 20 to the left of N and another number to the right of N.
3. Write a number from 21 to 30 to the left of G and another number to the right of G.
4. Write a number from 31 to 40 to the left of L and another number to the right of L.
5. Write a number from 41 to 50 to the left of I and another number to the right of I.
6. Write a number from 51 to 60 to the left of S and another number to the right of S.
7. Write a number from 61 to 70 to the left of H and another number to the right of H.

_____E_____

_____N_____

_____G_____

_____L_____

_____I_____

_____S_____

_____H_____

**Your teacher will say some numbers. Put an X on your number if the teacher says it. When you have 6 Xs, say, "I win!"**

## 7

**Don't write it. Don't say it.**
**Student A, come to the front of the class. Think of a letter. Don't write it. Don't say it. Other students, guess the secret letter. Ask only six questions.**

B: Is it before __f__?
A: Yes, it is./No, it isn't.
C: Is it after ____?
A: Yes, it is./No, it isn't.
D: Is it ____?
A: Yes, it is./No, it isn't.

a b c d e f g h i j k l m n o p q r s t u v w x y z

Unit 6  But they're expensive...

## 1

**Listen to the conversation and practice with a partner. Talk about the clothes in the picture. Use sentences like these:**

A: *This shirt is* nice, but *it's small/large.*
B: You're right.
A: *These sweaters are* nice, but *they're expensive.*
B: Not really.

S = small
M = medium
L = large
XL = extra large

## 2

**Listen and say these colors:**

white   yellow   orange   red   blue   green   brown   black

gray   pink   purple

## 3

**Work with a partner. Ask and answer questions like these:**

A: What color are the *sweaters* at *Miller's*?
B: They're *green, yellow, and blue.*
B: What color are the *dresses* at *Stacy's*?
A: They're *blue, red, and yellow.*

## 4

**Listen to the conversation and practice with a partner.**

CLERK: May I help you?
JOE: Yes, please. I'm looking for a gift for my *sister*. It's *her* birthday.
CLERK: How old is *she*?
JOE: *She's 16.*
CLERK: *Sixteen.* Well, *these headphones are popular.*
JOE: How much *are they*?
CLERK: *$49.00.*
JOE: Hmm. That's *expensive*.

**Have similar conversations with a partner.**

   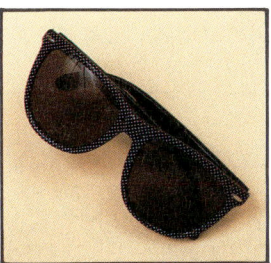

1. father/43
   gloves/warm
   $7.00/reasonable

2. girlfriend/18
   necklace/beautiful
   $26.00/expensive

3. grandfather/65
   slippers/comfortable
   $19.00/expensive

4. aunt/31
   sunglasses/cute
   $14.00/reasonable

5. grandmother/62
   scarves/beautiful
   $24.00/expensive

6. friend/17
   pocketbook/attractive
   $29.00/reasonable

7. brother/12
   watch/good-looking
   $15.00/reasonable

8. mother/41
   perfume/lovely
   $38.00/expensive

## 5

**Work with a partner. Buy a birthday gift for a friend or family member. Use the conversation in Part 4 and the items on these two pages.**

| GRAMMAR | | | | | | |
|---|---|---|---|---|---|---|
| This shirt | is | nice. | What color | is | it? | |
| It | 's | expensive. | | are | the sweaters? | |
| That | | | | | they? | |
| These shirts | are | reasonable. | | | | |
| They | 're | | | | | |

| USEFUL LANGUAGE |
|---|
| May I help you? |
| Yes, please. |
| I'm looking for a gift for my sister. |
| It's her birthday. |

Unit 7  Are you all right?

**Listen to the conversation and practice with a partner.**

GRANDMA: Hi, Jean.
JEAN: Oh, hi, Grandma.
GRANDMA: Are you all right?
JEAN: Yes, I'm fine.
GRANDMA: *Are* your *cats* all right?
JEAN: *Yes, they are.*
GRANDMA: That's good. *Is* your *piano* all right?
JEAN: *Yes, it is.*
GRANDMA: That's good. *Is* your *garden* all right?
JEAN: *No, it isn't. It's in bad shape.*
GRANDMA: That's too bad. And *are* your *bikes* all right?
JEAN: *No, they aren't.*
GRANDMA: Oh, I'm sorry.

**Have similar conversations with a partner.**

1. GRANDMA: Tell me about your *sister.*
   *Is her stereo* all right?
   JEAN: No, _____.

| | | | |
|---|---|---|---|
| sister | 2. parents | 3. brother | 4. other brother |
| stereo | painting | motorcycle | books |
| records | computer | skis | fish |
| guitar | rug | basketball | tape recorder |

18

## 2

**Listen to the conversation and practice with a partner.**

JOE: Hi, *Frank*. How are you? Come in.
FRANK: Thanks, but I'm in a hurry. Say, *are* my *glasses* here?
JOE: I don't know. Just a minute.

JOE: Ellen?
ELLEN: Yes?
JOE: It's *Frank*. *Are his glasses* here?
ELLEN: *His glasses?* No, *they aren't*.

JOE: *They aren't* here. Maybe *they're in your car*.
FRANK: Hmm. Maybe. Well, thanks. See you tomorrow.
JOE: OK, bye.

**Have similar conversations with a partner.**

1. Mrs. Connor
   gloves
   at school

2. Yoko and Tom
   keys
   at work

3. Roberto
   hat
   at school

4. Nick and Cindy
   calculator
   at work

## 3

**Use the conversation in Part 2. Work with two other students. They are Joe and Ellen. Ask them about your books and your _____.**

| GRAMMAR | | | | USEFUL LANGUAGE | |
|---|---|---|---|---|---|
| Is | your | piano | all right? | Hi. | Maybe. |
| Are | | cats | here? | Are you all right? | Thanks. |
| | | | | That's good. | See you tomorrow. |
| Yes, | it | is. | | That's too bad. | OK, bye. |
| | they | are. | | Oh, I'm sorry. | |
| | | | | Come in. | |
| No, | it | isn't. | | I'm in a hurry. | |
| | they | aren't. | | I don't know. | |
| | | | | Just a minute. | |
| at | school | | | | |
| | work | | | | |

Unit 8   What's the matter?

## 1

**Listen to the conversation and practice with a partner.**

A:  What's the matter? Are *you* OK?
B:  *I'm* fine. *I'm* just *thirsty*.

**Have similar conversations with a partner.**

1. you
   I/hot

2. you
   I/tired

3. you
   we/cold

4. they
   they/hungry

5. you
   we/busy

6. she
   she/nervous

7. you
   we/sleepy

8. they
   they/bored

## 2

**Listen to the conversation and practice with a partner.**

A:  Hi, _____. How are you?
          (name of partner)
B:  I'm OK. I'm just a little *bored*.
A:  Let's *go to the movies*.
B:  OK. Good idea.

**Use these words to make new conversations.**

| tired  | have lunch         |
| cold   | take a break       |
| bored  | have a cold drink  |
| hungry | go home            |
| hot    | go to the movies   |

# 3

**Listen to the conversation and practice with a partner.**

BETH: Hi. How are you this morning?
STEVEN: Not so good.
BETH: What's the matter? Are you sick?
STEVEN: No, no. I'm not sick. My test is today.
BETH: Today? What time?
STEVEN: It's at 10:30.
BETH: Oh. You're just nervous.
STEVEN: I'm not nervous!
BETH: But, Steven, look at your shoes! One is black and one is brown.
STEVEN: OK. I am nervous and very tired.

# 4

**Make your own questions and answers about the pictures. Use words from the box below.**

A: Is she *hot?*
B: Yes, she is.
A: Is she *happy?*
B: Yes, she is.
A: Is she *angry?*
B: No, she isn't.
A: Is she *thirsty?*
B: Maybe.

| Is | he / she | angry? happy? thirsty? hot? busy? sleepy? | Yes, | he / she | is. |
|---|---|---|---|---|---|
| Are | they | | | they | are. |
| | | | No, | he / she | isn't. |
| | | | | they | aren't. |

| GRAMMAR | | | | | | | | | USEFUL LANGUAGE |
|---|---|---|---|---|---|---|---|---|---|
| Is | he / she | tired? | Yes, | I | am. | No, | I | 'm not. | What's the matter?<br>Are you OK?<br>Not so good.<br>I'm \| just thirsty.<br>       \| just a little thirsty.<br>Let's go to the movies.<br>Good idea. |
| Are | you / they | | | he / she | is. | | he / she | isn't. | |
| | | | | we / they | are. | | we / they | aren't. | |

Unit 9   What's in the living room?

## 1

**Listen and say the names of these rooms and objects.**

| BEDROOM | BATHROOM | LIVING ROOM | KITCHEN |
|---|---|---|---|
| 1. bed | 7. sink | 12. sofa | 19. table |
| 2. dresser | 8. bathtub | 13. rug | 20. chairs |
| 3. mirror | 9. toilet | 14. chair | 21. stove |
| 4. umbrella | 10. newspaper | 15. TV | 22. refrigerator |
| 5. magazines | 11. cats | 16. desk | 23. sink |
| 6. kids | | 17. lamp | 24. phone |
| | | 18. phone books | 25. broom |
| | | | 26. keys |

**Work with a partner. Ask and answer questions like these:**

A:  What's in the bedroom?
B:  A bed, a dresser, and magazines.
A:  What's in the living room/bathroom/kitchen?

## 2

**Listen to the conversation and practice with a partner.**

A:  Where's the dog?
B:  It's *in front of* the sofa.

next to             on                under              behind

22

# 3

**Work with a partner. Ask and answer questions like these. Look at the picture in Part 1, and use the words from Part 2.**

A: *Is* the *broom* in the *kitchen?*
B: *Yes, it is. It's next to* the *sink.*

A: *Are* the *magazines* in the *living room?*
B: *No, they aren't. They're* in the *bedroom under* the *bed.*

1. TV/living room
2. lamp/bedroom
3. phone books/kitchen
4. cats/living room
5. umbrella/bedroom
6. kids/bathroom
7. rug/living room
8. newspaper/bathroom
9. phone/kitchen
10. keys/living room

# 4

**Work with a partner. Student A, look on the left. Student B, look on the right. A, ask B to draw 1, 3, 5, 7, and 9. B, ask A to draw 2, 4, 6, 8, and 10. Use this conversation:**

## STUDENT A

A: Draw a *chair in front of the desk.*

## STUDENT B

B: OK. (Draws a *chair in front of the desk.*)
B: Draw a *newspaper on the desk.*

| GRAMMAR | | | | | | USEFUL LANGUAGE |
|---|---|---|---|---|---|---|
| What's in the | bedroom? living room? | | It's | in front of next to on under behind | the sofa. | Here it is! |
| Where's the umbrella? | | | | | | |
| Is Are | the | broom brooms | in the kitchen? | | | |

Unit 10  Oh, yes—Room 307 is excellent.

## 1

**Listen to the conversation and practice with a partner.**

MANAGER: Oh, yes—Room 307 is excellent! There are two big, comfortable beds, and there's a wonderful view of the beach.
TOURIST: *Is* there *a phone* in the room?
MANAGER: Yes, there *'s one next to the bed.*
TOURIST: *Are* there *any glasses?*
MANAGER: Yes, there *are some in the bathroom.*

**Have similar conversations with a partner.**

1. extra blankets in the dresser
2. alarm clock on the table
3. telephone book on the table
4. air conditioner in the window

 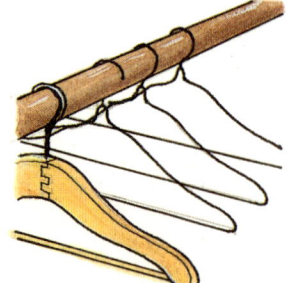  

5. extra pillows in the closet
6. hangers in the closet
7. TV set on the dresser
8. laundry bags in the closet

## 2

**Listen to the conversation and practice with a partner.**

A: Is there a *restaurant* in the hotel?
B: No, there isn't, but there's one nearby.

**Have similar conversations with a partner.**

1. swimming pool
2. ice machine
3. mailbox
4. coffee shop

## 3

**Listen to the conversation and practice with a partner.**

MANAGER: Hello?
TOURIST: Hello. This is Room *307*.
MANAGER: Oh, yes. May I help you?
TOURIST: Well, there's a problem with my room.
MANAGER: A problem? What's wrong?
TOURIST: *There's a mouse in the bathtub.*
MANAGER: *A mouse in the bathtub?*
TOURIST: Yes! Come and see.

| Room | Problems | Room | Problems |
|------|----------|------|----------|
| 307  | There's a mouse. | 416 | There are bugs. |
| 105  | There's no hot water. | 221 | There are no blankets. |

**Have similar conversations with a partner.**

1. 108
   no sheets on the bed

2. 205
   hole in the wall

3. 210
   bugs in the closet

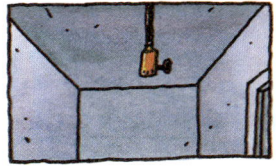
4. 301
   no lights in the hall

5. 614
   no soap in the bathroom

6. 517
   no towels in the closet

## 4

**Work with a partner. Ask and answer questions like these:**

A: What's wrong in your house/apartment?
B: There's *no air conditioner.*

| GRAMMAR | | | | | | | | USEFUL LANGUAGE |
|---------|---|---|---|---|---|---|---|---|
| There | 's | one | next to the bed. | There | 's | a bug. | | This is Room 307. |
|       | are | some |                  |       | are | bugs. | | There's a problem with my room. |
|       |    |     |                  |       |    | no bugs. | | What's wrong? |
| Is | there | a blanket | in the room? | | | | | Come and see. |
| Are |      | any blankets |            | | | | | |

25

Summary 2  Units 6–10

## 1

**Look at the picture. Then listen and write the letter.**

1. F     2. ___
3. ___   4. ___
5. ___   6. ___
7. ___   8. ___
9. ___  10. ___
11. ___ 12. ___
13. ___ 14. ___
15. ___ 16. ___

## 2

**Listen and circle the letter of the best answer.**

a. Yes, it is.
(b.) Yes, they are.

1. a. How are you?
   b. OK. Good-bye.

2. a. It's $14.50.
   b. They're $14.50.

3. a. They're in the car.
   b. It's on the table.

4. a. Thanks, but I'm in a hurry.
   b. You're welcome.

5. a. Let's play tennis.
   b. Let's have a cold drink.

6. a. There are bugs in our bed.
   b. There's a table in the kitchen.

7. a. No, there aren't.
   b. Oh, what's wrong?

8. a. No, it's very small.
   b. No, thanks. I'm tired.

9. a. I'm just happy.
   b. I'm very nervous.

10. a. Yes, there are.
    b. Yes, there is.

11. a. It's very expensive.
    b. They're very expensive.

12. a. It's $19.00.
    b. It's very comfortable.

26

Work with a partner for Parts 3 and 4. Student A, look at this page. Student B, look at the next page.

# STUDENT A

## 3

**What is it? Listen and write the letter.**

1. C  
2. ____  
3. ____  
4. ____  
5. ____  
6. ____  

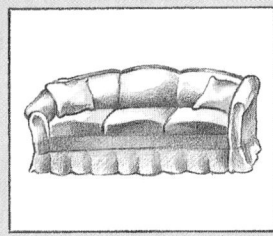 A ___sofa___

 B ___door___

 C _____

 D _____

E _____

 F ___air conditioner___

**Work with a partner. Write the missing words. Use this conversation:**

A: What's the word for *A*?

B: It's a *sofa*.
A: Right.

B: Spell it, please.
A: S-O-F-A.

B: I don't know.
A: It's a *sofa*.

## 4

**Student A, start the conversation. Then listen to your partner and choose a good answer. Continue the conversation. Then try the conversation again. Choose different answers.**

—How's Emma?

—Are there any nice gifts in the shop?
—Is there a swimming pool next to it?

—Is there a nice view from the living room?
—Are there any pocketbooks?

—What's the problem?
—Where's the gift shop?

—No closets? Where are her clothes?
—Is that the hotel next to the beach?

# STUDENT B

## 3
**What is it? Listen and write the letter.**

1. C    2. ____    3. ____
4. ____   5. ____    6. ____

A _____

B _____

C    table

D    refrigerator

E    bathtub

F _____

**Work with a partner. Write the missing words. Use this conversation:**

A: What's the word for *A*?

B: It's a *sofa*.
A: Right.

B: I don't know.
A: It's a *sofa*.

B: Spell it, please.
A: S-O-F-A.

## 4
**Student B, listen to your partner and then choose a good answer. Continue the conversation. Then try the conversation again. Choose different answers.**

—She's fine, and her new apartment is very nice.
—She's tired, but her new gift shop is wonderful.

—Yes. It's very big.
—Yes. The scarves, the gloves, and the necklaces are nice.

—Oh, yes. The pocketbooks are attractive, too.
—Yes, but there's a problem with the apartment.

—It's in the Grand Hotel.
—There are no closets.

—Under the bed.
—Yes, it is.

## 5 What is it?

Team A gives clues for the names of things in the picture. Team B finds the things and gives the name. After three questions, the teams change parts.

TEAM A STUDENT: They're *$6.00*.
TEAM B STUDENT: The *sunglasses*.
TEAM A STUDENT: That's right.

TEAM A STUDENT: It's *under the window*.
TEAM B STUDENT: The *dog*.
TEAM A STUDENT: Sorry, that isn't right.

**Use these words in your clues:**

| next to | in front of | small | under |
| on the right | large | on | on the left |
| tall | in | $_____ | expensive |

**Make clues for these things:**

| door | dog | clock | sunglasses |
| window | chair | gloves | watches |
| woman | table | necklaces | book |
| cat | pillows | scarves | pen |
| mirror | painting | doll | rug |

Unit 11   By the way, how much is it?

# 1

**Listen and say the prices.**

**Work with a partner. Student A, read the prices on the left. Student B, write the prices that Student A reads. Student B, read the prices on the right. Student A, write those prices.**

## STUDENT A                                        STUDENT B

$ 3.00   $10.00    _____  _____     _____  _____    $  .99   $45.89
$  .42   $ 8.75    _____  _____     _____  _____    $31.65   $26.00
$77.50   $22.99    _____  _____     _____  _____    $ 5.00   $91.90

# 2

**Listen to the conversation and practice with a partner.**

A: How much is *an orange drink* over there?
B: *Sixty-five cents.*
A: Oh, that's *expensive*. It's *fifty cents* here.

B: How much are the *hot dogs* over there?
A: *Seventy-five cents.*
B: Oh, that's *cheap*. It's *eighty-five cents* here.

**Have similar conversations with a partner. Student A, look at Bob's menu. Student B, look at Joe's menu. A, ask B about Joe's. B, ask A about Bob's.**

## 3

**Listen to the conversation and practice with a partner.**

A: May I help you?
B: Yes, please. I'd like *a jacket*.
A: *Jackets* are over there.

B: *This is* nice, but *it's* too big.
A: Let's see. Try *this*.
B: Oh, this size is good, but *is* there *a green one?*

A: Let's see. Here you are.
B: Thanks. By the way, how much *is it?*
A: *$99.99.*
B: *$99.99?* That's too expensive!

**Have similar conversations with a partner.**

1. some boots
   any gray ones?
   $95.99

2. blouse
   pink
   $59.95

3. slippers
   brown
   $32.00

4. bathrobe
   blue
   $54.99

5. running shoes
   white
   $70.00

6. socks
   yellow
   $10.99

6. suit
   black
   $98.99

8. bathing suit
   purple
   $65.95

| GRAMMAR | | | | | | USEFUL LANGUAGE |
|---|---|---|---|---|---|---|
| How much is | an | orange drink? | | It's | too big. | Over there. |
| | a | hot dog? | | They're | | Here. |
| I'd like | | pretzel. | | | | That's expensive./cheap. |
| | | | | | | Here you are. |
| Is | there | a | green | one? | | Let's see. |
| Are | | any | | ones? | | By the way... |

Unit 12  Go one block to Maple Avenue.

**1**  Listen and say the names of the places on the map. Then practice the names with a partner.

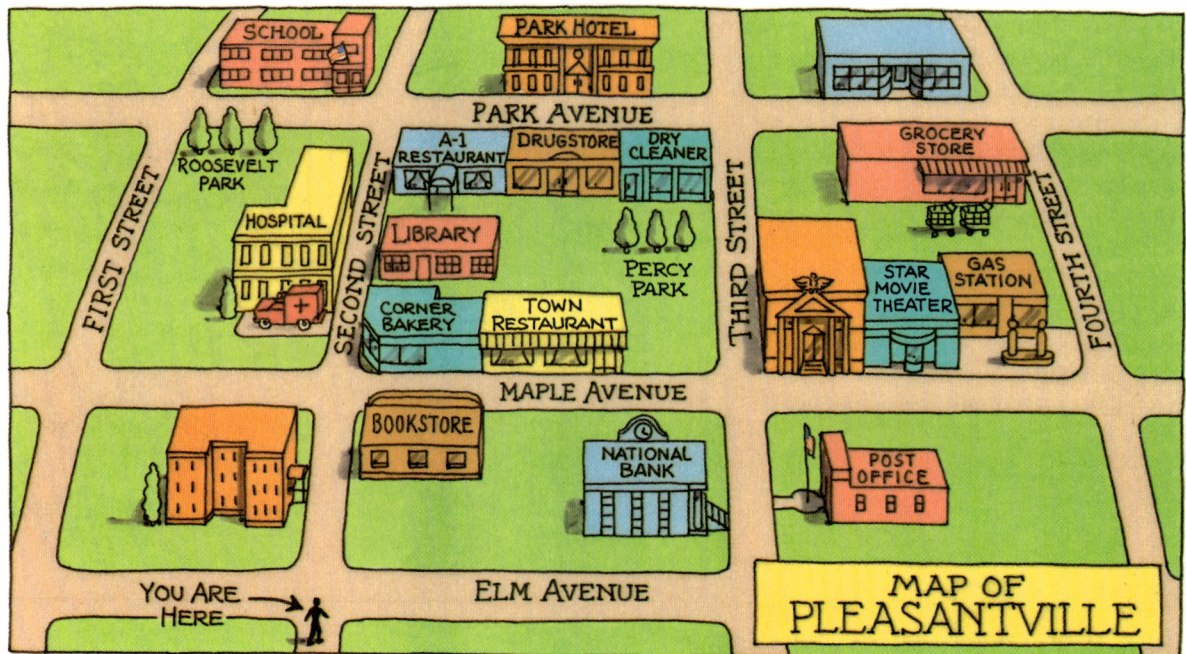

**2** Listen and find the places on the map. Then practice with a partner.

A: Where's the bookstore?
B: On Maple Avenue across from the bakery.
A: Where's the drugstore?
B: On Park Avenue between the restaurant and the dry cleaner.
A: Where's the A-1 Restaurant?
B: On Park Avenue next to the drugstore.
A: Where's the gas station?
B: On the corner of Maple Avenue and Fourth Street.
A: Where's the school?
B: Between First Street and Second Street on Park Avenue in the middle of the block.

**Have similar conversations with a partner. Look at the map again.**

1. dry cleaner
   drugstore

2. bookstore
   Maple Avenue/
   Second Street

3. hospital
   library

4. grocery store
   Third Street/
   Fourth Street

5. Park Hotel
   Second Street/
   Third Street

6. Corner Bakery
   bookstore

7. A-1 Restaurant
   Second Street/
   Park Avenue

8. National Bank
   post office

**3** Work with a partner. Draw a map of a neighborhood on a piece of paper. Write the names of the places on the map. Then ask and answer ten questions about the map.

## 4

Look at Map 1. Put your finger on the . Follow the directions with your teacher. Then practice with a partner.

- Go one block to Maple Avenue. Turn right. Go to the bookstore.
- Start again at the 🚶. Go two blocks to Park Avenue. Turn left. Go to the school. It's on the right.
- Start again at the 🚶. Go straight and cross Maple Avenue. Go to the hospital. It's on the left.

## 5

Look at Map 1 again. Listen to the conversation and practice with a partner. Start at the 🚶.

A: Excuse me, please. Is *the Corner Bakery* in this area?
B: Yes. It's *on Maple Avenue across from the bookstore.*
A: Where's that?
B: Go *one block* on *Second Street* to *Maple Avenue.*
A: *One block?*
B: Yes. Then *turn right.*
A: Uh-huh. *Turn right.*
B: The *Corner Bakery* is *on the corner on the left.*
A: OK, thanks a lot!

## 6

Work with a partner. Student A, look at Map 1 and ask Student B about the places on the left. Student B, look at Map 2 and ask Student A about the places on the right. Practice the conversation from Part 5.

**STUDENT A**
1. the Park Avenue bakery
3. the Gold Star Hotel
5. the American Bank

**STUDENT B**
2. the Town Restaurant
4. Percy Park
6. the Star Movie Theater

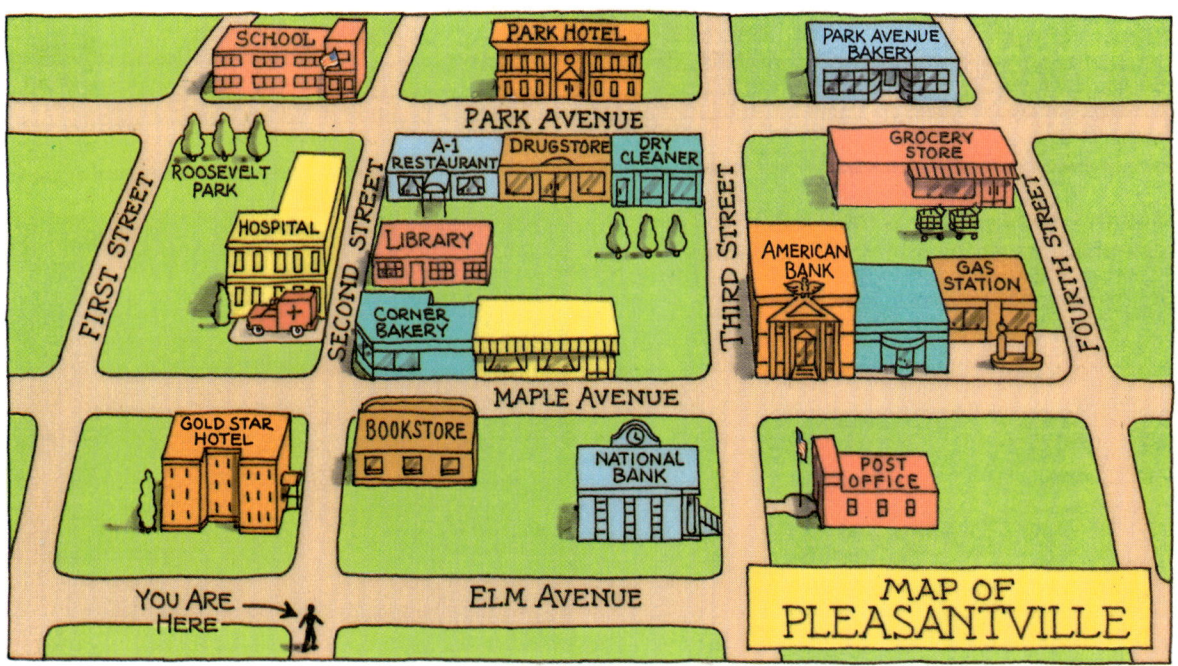

33

Unit 13  What's happening?

## 1

 **Listen to the conversation and practice with a partner.**

A: What *are you* doing?
B: *I'm studying.*
A: Really? What *are you studying?*
B: *English.*

**Have similar conversations with a partner.**

1. your sister
   painting
   a picture

2. father
   writing
   a letter

3. grandparents
   reading
   the newspaper

4. your brother and his
   wife
   playing
   basketball

5. little brother
   cooking
   chicken soup

6. mother
   eating
   my brother's chicken
   soup

## 2

**Say the names of the places in Part 1. Then ask and answer questions with a partner.**

A: Where *are you studying?*
B: In the *dining room.*

| WHO | PLACE |
|---|---|
| you | dining room |
| father | |
| little brother | |
| brother and wife | |
| sister | |
| grandparents | |
| mother | |

34

**3** Look at the picture and listen to the conversation. Practice the conversation with a partner. Then cover the conversation and tell what's happening in the park.

FRANK: Our news helicopter is flying over Central Park. Let's talk to Sue Green, our reporter. Sue? Are you listening, Sue?

SUE: Yes, I'm listening, Frank. I'm flying 300 feet over the park. It's the first day of spring. It's a beautiful day, and people are really enjoying it. Old people, young people...

FRANK: Tell me, what's happening?

SUE: Well, Frank, children are running with balloons. People are eating hot dogs and ice cream by the lake. In front of the fountain, musicians are playing, and people are listening to the music.

FRANK: That's great.

SUE: And Frank, a man is watching TV under a tree.

FRANK: Are you kidding? He's watching TV in the park?

SUE: Yes, look! He's watching this program. Look! He's waving.

| GRAMMAR | | | | | | | USEFUL LANGUAGE |
|---|---|---|---|---|---|---|---|
| What | is<br>'s | he<br>she | studying? | I | 'm | studying English. | What's happening?<br>That's great.<br>Are you kidding? |
| Where | are | you<br>they | | He<br>She | 's | | |
| | | | | You<br>We<br>They | 're | | |

Unit 14   Is she going to classes this week?

## 1

**Listen to the conversation and practice with a partner.**

A:  She isn't going to classes this week. Why?  
A:  Oh.

B:  Because she's visiting a friend in London.

**Work with a partner. A, ask B, about the pictures on the left. B, choose the best answer from the pictures on the right.**

### STUDENT A            STUDENT B

1. He/eat in restaurants/summer

take eight classes

2. You/work in the supermarket/semester

save money for college

3. They/go to bed late/semester

stay with their grandmother

4. She/take care of her kids/week

go to school early

## 2

**Work with a partner. Ask and answer questions about the pictures in Part 1.**

A:  *Is she going to classes* this *week?*  
B:  No, she isn't. She's visiting a friend in London.

## 3

Ask two other students what they're doing this week.

| ARE YOU | Name _Maria_ (Student 1) | Name _John_ (Student 2) |
|---|---|---|
| ...working? | ✓ | |
| ...watching a lot of TV? | | |
| ...saving money? | | ✓ |
| ...eating in restaurants a lot? | | |

## 4

Listen to the conversation and practice with a partner.

TONY: Ray? Is that you?
RAY: Oh, Tony! It's great to see you.
TONY: What's happening with you this year? You aren't studying in the library. Are you taking classes?
RAY: No, I'm working full-time. I'm just taking English. What about you?
TONY: I'm finishing college this year, so I'm spending all my time in the library.
RAY: How many classes are you taking?
TONY: Eight! But they're going well.
RAY: So where are you living now?
TONY: With my family. The dormitory is too expensive.
RAY: I know. I'm living with my family, too. Oh, my class is starting now. It was nice seeing you.
TONY: Thanks, Ray. Good-bye.

**A friend, Mia, asks about Ray.**

MIA: What's happening with Ray this year? He isn't studying in the library. Is he taking classes?
TONY: No, he's _____.

**A friend, Alice, asks about Tony.**

ALICE: What's happening with Tony this year?
RAY: He's _____.

| GRAMMAR | | | | | | | USEFUL LANGUAGE |
|---|---|---|---|---|---|---|---|
| I | 'm | visiting a friend in London. | Am | I | visiting a friend in London? | | Why? |
| | 'm not | | Is | he | | | Because . . . |
| He | 's | | | she | | | It's great to see you. |
| She | isn't | | Are | you | | | What about you? |
| You | 're | | | we | | | They're/It's going well. |
| We | | | | they | | | Good luck! |
| They | aren't | | | | | | |

Unit 15   Don't forget your keys!

## 1

Listen to the conversation and practice with a partner.

1. A: Whose ball is this? Is it yours?
   B: No, it's not mine. It's hers.

2. A: Whose _____?
   B: No, _____

3. A: Whose _____?
   B: No, _____

4. A: Whose _____?
   B: Yes, it's ours. We're very sorry, sir. Here's some money for the window.

## 2

Listen to the conversations and practice with a partner. Student A, look only at Sam and Janet. Student B, look only at Ken and Sue.

A: What color is *Ken's* sweater?
B: *His* is *white*.

A: What color are *Ken's and Sue's* pants?
B: *His* are black and *hers* are yellow.

B: What color are *Sam's and Janet's* shoes?
A: *Theirs* are *both blue*.

### STUDENT A                    ### STUDENT B

**Now ask about these:** dress, scarf, shirt, socks, necklace, and glasses.

## 3

**Practice the conversation with a partner.**

SAM: Don't forget your *keys!*
SUE: *They're* not mine.
SAM: Oh. Whose *are they?*
SUE: I don't know. Maybe *they're* my *father's.* Yes, *they're his.* Here's *his* name.

**Have similar conversations with a partner.**

1. books
   girlfriend's

2. jacket
   sister's

3. ball
   brother's

4. camera
   parents'

5. pitchers
   mother's

6. wallet
   boyfriend's

7. pen
   grandmother's

8. watch
   uncle's

| GRAMMAR | | | | | | | | | USEFUL LANGUAGE |
|---|---|---|---|---|---|---|---|---|---|
| Whose ball is this? | | | | | | | | | We're very sorry, sir. |
| | | | | | | | | | Don't forget your keys. |
| It | 's | mine. | Is it | mine? | Mine | is | | brown. | |
| | 's not | yours. | | yours? | Yours | are | | | |
| | | his. | | his? | His | | | | |
| | | hers. | | hers? | Hers | | | | |
| | | ours. | | ours? | Ours | | | | |
| | | theirs. | | theirs? | Theirs | | | | |

Summary 3  Units 11–15

## 1

**Listen to the sentences. Each sentence gives directions for one place on the map. Write the letter of the place.**

1. E    2. ____    3. ____    4. ____
5. ____   6. ____    7. ____    8. ____
9. ____   10. ____

## 2

**Listen and circle the letter of the best answer.**

a. Thanks a lot. (circled)
b. Same here.

1. a. I don't know.
   b. That's expensive.

2. a. On the table.
   b. It's John's.

3. a. I'm not hungry.
   b. I'm very hungry.

4. a. With my friend, John.
   b. I'm going to the library.

5. a. What's she painting?
   b. Yes, please.

6. a. She's watching TV.
   b. She's fine.

7. a. No, it's red.
   b. No, it's mine.

8. a. Yes, there is. It's in the dining room.
   b. Yes, there is. It's next to the school.

9. a. Sixty-five cents.
   b. I'd like one, please.

10. a. Yellow. What's yours?
    b. Monday. What's yours?

11. a. No, he's working at a Japanese restaurant.
    b. Because he's saving money for college.

12. a. Let's see. Try this big one.
    b. Let's see. Try this white one.

40

Work with a partner for Parts 3 and 4. Student A, look at this page. Student B, look at the next page.

# STUDENT A

## 3

Listen to the conversations. Write the time, price, and directions for the activities.

1. sumo wrestling
   Time: _____
   Price: $25.00
   Directions: _____
   _____

2. The Nutcracker Ballet
   Time: 8:00
   Price: _____
   Directions: Park Avenue between 10th and 11th Streets

3. guitar concert
   Time: 6:00
   Price: _____
   Directions: 19th Street, next to the art museum

4. International Tango Contest
   Time: _____
   Price: $6.00
   Directions: _____
   _____

Check your answers with your partner. Start like this:

A: Is the *sumo wrestling* at *7:00?*
B: Yes, that's right./No, it's at _____.
   Is it *$25.00?*
A: Yes, that's right./No, it's _____.
   Is it *on Third Avenue across from Blackman Park?*
B: _____

**Student A, you want to go out tonight with Student B, but you only have $10.00. Where are you going? Talk to Student B. Start like this:**

A: Let's go to _____.
B: OK./No, it's too expensive.

## 4

**Student A, start the conversation. Then listen to your partner and choose a good answer. Continue the conversation. Then try the conversation again. Choose different answers.**

—I'm going to Lacy's Department Store.

—Well, it's a good store.
—A rain hat.

—I know, but it's too small.
—I know, but there's a big sale this week.

—OK, thanks. Say, this is a nice one.
—A tie.

—What? Mine?
—Orange. But I'm not buying an orange tie.

—That's very nice. Thanks a lot.
—I'd like a purple one.

# STUDENT B

## 3

**Listen to the conversations. Write the time, price, and directions for the activities.**

1. sumo wrestling
   Time: 7:00
   Price: _____
   Directions: On Third Avenue across from Blackman Park

2. The Nutcracker Ballet
   Time: _____
   Price: $35.00
   Directions: _____
   _____

3. guitar concert
   Time: _____
   Price: $12.00
   Directions: _____
   _____

4. International Tango Contest
   Time: 7:45
   Price: _____
   Directions: Across from Stevens Hospital

**Check your answers with your partner. Start like this:**

A: Is the *sumo wrestling* at *7:00*?
B: Yes, that's right./No, it's at _____.
   Is it *$25.00*?
A: Yes, that's right./No, it's _____.
   Is it *on Third Avenue across from Blackman Park*?
B: _____

**Student B, you want to go out tonight with Student A after 7:30. Where are you going? Talk to Student A. Start like this:**

A: Let's go to _____.
B: OK./No, it's too early.

## 4

**Student B, listen to your partner and then choose a good answer. Continue the conversation. Then try the conversation again. Choose different answers.**

—What are you looking for?
—Why are you going to Lacy's?

—You're wearing a rain hat!
—Yes, but it's too expensive.

—What are you looking for?
—Here. Try mine.

—A tie? What's your favorite color?
—It's yours.

—Yes. I'm giving it to you. It's too big for me.
—What color are you looking for?

—You're kidding!
—You're welcome.

## 5

**Use the map on page 40. Listen to your teacher give directions from the X on the map. Practice like this:**

TEACHER: Where are you?
STUDENT A: On the corner of _____ and _____.

**Student A, give directions like this to the class:**

A: Go one block to Second Avenue. Turn left. It's between Store E and Store F. Where are you?
CLASS: At the apartments.

**Use these words.**

| | |
|---|---|
| Go _____ block(s) to _____ St./Ave. | next to |
| Cross/Don't cross the street. | across from |
| Go straight. | between _____ and _____ |
| in the middle of the block | Turn right. |
| at the corner of _____ and _____ | Turn left. |
| Stop. | |

## 6

**Ask and answer with a partner.**

A: *What's your favorite city?*
B: *Bombay.*

**Tell the class about your partner.**

A: _____'s favorite *city* is *Bombay.*
   (Name of partner)

**Listen to other students tell about their partners. Write the information about four students in the class.**

Unit 16  Do you need a racket?

## 1

**Lucy and Sara are buying things for tennis lessons. Listen to the conversation and practice with a partner.**

LUCY:  Let's see. I have *tennis shoes.*
SARA:  I have *tennis shoes,* too.
LUCY:  I need a *shirt.*
SARA:  I have a *shirt.*
LUCY:  I _____.

**Now you and your partner are Lucy and Sara. Continue the conversation.**

|  | HAVE | | NEED | |
|---|---|---|---|---|
|  | Lucy | Sara | Lucy | Sara |
| tennis shoes | ✓ | ✓ |  |  |
| shirt |  | ✓ | ✓ |  |
| socks |  |  | ✓ | ✓ |
| sunglasses | ✓ | ✓ |  |  |
| sunscreen |  |  | ✓ | ✓ |
| hat |  | ✓ | ✓ |  |
| tennis balls | ✓ |  |  | ✓ |
| racket |  | ✓ | ✓ |  |

## 2

**Listen to the conversation and practice with a partner.**

LUCY:  Excuse me, do you have tennis equipment?
SALESMAN:  Yes, we do. Over here. Do you need *any tennis balls?*
LUCY:  *No,* I *don't,* thanks. I have *some good ones* at home.
SALESMAN:  Do you need *a racket?*
LUCY:  *Yes,* and I want *a good one.*

**Practice the conversation about all the equipment in Part 1 with a partner. Answer for Lucy. Then change roles and answer for Sara.**

SALESMAN:  Do you need *any socks?*
LUCY:  *Yes,* I *do.* I want *some good ones.*

## 3

**You are going on a trip to Florida. Make a list, things you "have" and another list, things you "need." Then talk about your lists with a partner. Use the conversations in Parts 1 and 2.**

## 4

**Listen to the conversation and practice with a partner.**

SARA: Lucy, let's take a break. I need a drink. Do you want one?
LUCY: Sure.
SARA: There's a vending machine over there.

SARA: There's orange, apple, grape, or tomato juice. What do you want?
LUCY: *Orange* juice.
SARA: And I want *grape juice.* Oh, no! I don't have change. I only have a *five*-dollar bill.
LUCY: (Looking in purse) I have a lot of change.

LUCY: Let's see. It's fifty cents. You want *grape* juice, right?
SARA: Yes, thanks.
LUCY: Here. And I want *orange juice.*
SARA: Now let's relax.

**Have similar conversations with a partner. You're at the vending machine. Start like this:** There's orange, apple . . .

1. John   Tom
   apple  tomato

2. Harry  Cathy
   grape  apple

3. Cindy   Doug
   tomato  orange

4. Anne   George
   apple  tomato

| GRAMMAR | | | | | | | USEFUL LANGUAGE |
|---|---|---|---|---|---|---|---|
| I | need | a shirt. | | Do you | need | any shorts? | Sure. |
| | have | tennis shoes. | | | have | | What do you want? |
| | want | | | | want | | I have change. |
| | | | | | | | Let's relax. |
| Yes, | I | do. | | I | want | one. | |
| No, | | don't. | | | | a good one. | |
| | | | | | | some good ones. | |

45

Unit 17    Do you like baseball?

## 1

**Listen to the conversation and practice with a partner.**

PAT: Do you like *baseball*?
SANDY: Oh, yes! I love it!
PAT: There's a good *game* at *3:00*. Let's go together.
SANDY: OK. Good idea!

**Have similar conversations with a partner.**

1. football game/7:15
2. soccer game/4:00
3. wrestling tournament/4:30
4. jazz concert/7:00

5. classical music concert/7:30
6. rock and roll concert/7:15
7. modern art exhibit/2:30
8. tennis tournament/5:00

## 2

**Work with a partner. Ask and answer questions like this:**

A: Do you like *jazz*?
B: Yes, I like it | a lot.
                 | pretty much.
                 | now and then.
   I don't really like it.

**Now ask about these:** rock and roll, skiing, football, wrestling, opera, and ballet.

46

## 3

**Listen to the conversation and practice with a partner.**

SANDY: Hi! Are you ready for the game?
PAT: Now? The game is at 3:00 and it's only *1:00*.
SANDY: *I* know, but *I* want a good *seat* at the game.
PAT: Oh. OK. Do you want a sandwich?
SANDY: No, thanks. *I* really want *a hot dog* at the game.
PAT: Really?
SANDY: *I* love *hot dogs*—but only at ball games.
PAT: Well, I don't like *hot dogs*. I need a sandwich before the game.
SANDY: OK. But please hurry.
PAT: I know. You want a good *seat*.

**Have similar conversations with partners.**

1. Anna and Vicki
   1:15
   view
   french fries

2. Lisa and Mary
   1:30
   parking spot
   hamburgers

| GRAMMAR | | | | |
|---|---|---|---|---|
| Do you | like | baseball? | | |
|  | want | a sandwich? | | |
| Yes, | I | | like it | a lot. |
|  | we | | | pretty much. |
|  |  | | | now and then. |
| No, |  | don't. | | |

USEFUL LANGUAGE

I love it!
Let's go together.
Are you ready?
Please hurry.

Unit 18  Are you ready to order?

## 1

**Listen to the conversation and practice with a partner.**

A: It's *12:30*. Do you want some *lunch?*
B: I don't really want *lunch*, but I'd like some *ice cream*.

**Have similar conversations with a partner.**

1. 8:30/breakfast
   coffee
2. 6:30/dinner
   salad
3. 7:15/breakfast
   juice
4. 1:30/lunch
   soup

5. 7:45/breakfast
   tea
6. 5:45/dinner
   pie
7. 12:15/lunch
   cake
8. 8:15/dinner
   yogurt

## 2

**Listen to the conversation and practice with a partner.**

WAITER: Are you ready to order?
CUSTOMER: Yes. I'd like some *ice cream*, please.
WAITER: What kind of *ice cream* would you like?
CUSTOMER: Uh . . . *chocolate*, please.
WAITER: I'm sorry. We don't have any *chocolate* today.
CUSTOMER: Oh. That's too bad. Do you have any *vanilla ice cream?*
WAITER: Yes, we do.
CUSTOMER: OK. I'd like that, please.
WAITER: Would you like anything to drink?
CUSTOMER: Yes. Some *iced coffee*, please.

**Have similar conversations with a partner.**

1. soup
   chicken
   onion soup
   lemonade

2. yogurt
   blueberry
   plain yogurt
   tea

3. cake
   chocolate
   carrot cake
   orange juice

4. pie
   lemon
   apple pie
   coffee

5. salad
   spinach
   carrot salad
   iced tea

6. soup
   tomato
   vegetable soup
   milk

48

**3** Student A, you are the waiter or waitress. Look at your menu for today. The restaurant is not serving some foods today. Student B, you are the customer. Look at the menu and order. Use the conversation in Part 2. Then change roles.

### STUDENT A

### STUDENT B

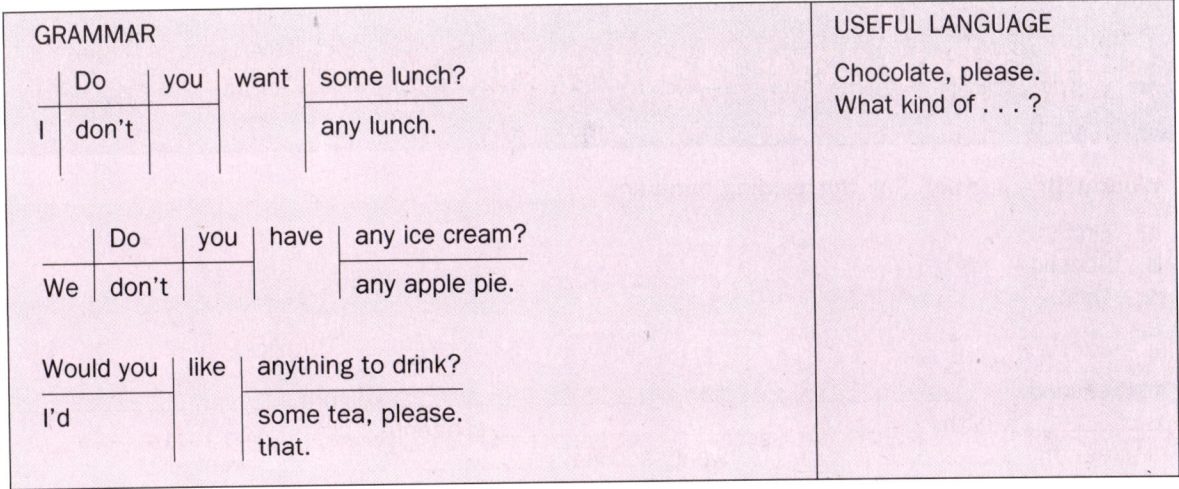

| GRAMMAR | | | |
|---|---|---|---|
| | Do | you | want | some lunch? |
| I | don't | | | any lunch. |

| | Do | you | have | any ice cream? |
|---|---|---|---|---|
| We | don't | | | any apple pie. |

| | Would you | like | anything to drink? |
|---|---|---|---|
| | I'd | | some tea, please. |
| | | | that. |

USEFUL LANGUAGE

Chocolate, please.
What kind of . . . ?

Unit 19   Is that one-way or round-trip?

## 1

**Listen to the conversation and practice with a partner. Look at the train schedule.**

CUSTOMER: My *sister wants* to arrive in *Washington, D.C.* by *3:30* P.M. What time *does she* need to leave here?
AGENT: At *12:25*.
CUSTOMER: *12:25*. OK. How much is a one-way ticket, please?
AGENT: It's *$43.00*.
CUSTOMER: My *parents* want to arrive in *Boston* by *7:00* P.M. What time *do they* need to leave here?
AGENT: At *2:00*.
CUSTOMER: *2:00*. OK. How much is a one-way ticket, please?
AGENT: It's *$25.50*.

### AMTREX TRAIN SCHEDULE

| DEPART: NEW YORK, NY | 12:00 P.M. | 12:24 P.M. | 2:00 P.M. | 3:00 P.M. | 6:55 P.M. | 8:20 P.M. |
|---|---|---|---|---|---|---|
| ARRIVE: BOSTON, MA | 4:50 P.M. | 5:15 P.M. | 6:45 P.M. | 7:45 P.M. | 9:30 P.M. | 11:35 P.M. |
| DEPART: NEW YORK, NY | 8:30 A.M. | 12:25 P.M. | 6:30 P.M. | | | |
| ARRIVE: WASHINGTON, D.C. | 11:22 A.M. | 3:15 P.M. | 9:50 P.M. | | | |

**Have similar conversations with a partner.**

1. neighbors
   Boston
   8:00 P.M.
   $33.00

2. daughter
   Boston
   5:00 P.M.
   $33.00

3. friends
   Washington, D.C.
   noon
   $43.00

4. grandparents
   Washington, D.C.
   11:45 A.M.
   $43.00

## 2

**Listen to the months of the year and the dates. Practice them with a partner.**

January, February, March, April, May, June, July, August, September, October, November, December

| 1st first | 2nd second | 3rd third | 4th fourth | 5th fifth | 6th sixth | 7th seventh | 8th eighth |
|---|---|---|---|---|---|---|---|
| 9th ninth | 10th tenth | 11th eleventh | 12th twelfth | 13th thirteenth | 14th fourteenth | 15th fifteenth | 16th sixteenth |
| 17th seventeenth | 18th eighteenth | 19th nineteenth | 20th twentieth | 21st twenty-first | 22nd twenty-second | 23rd twenty-third | 24th twenty-fourth |
| 25th twenty-fifth | 26th twenty-sixth | 27th twenty-seventh | 28th twenty-eighth | 29th twenty-ninth | 30th thirtieth | 31st thirty-first | |

**Work with a partner. Say the missing numbers.**

A: First.
B: Second.
A: Third.
B: _____

first, second, _____, _____, fifth, _____, _____, eighth, _____, _____, _____, twelfth, _____, _____, _____, sixteenth, _____, _____, nineteenth, _____, _____, twenty-second, _____, _____, twenty-fifth

## 3

**Listen to the conversation and practice with a partner.**

AGENT: May I help you?
CUSTOMER: Yes, please. I'd like to buy a ticket to *Manila* for *myself*.
AGENT: When would *you* like to leave?
CUSTOMER: *July 2nd*.
AGENT: We have a flight at *7:15 P.M.*
CUSTOMER: Do you have anything in the *morning*?
AGENT: No, I'm sorry.
CUSTOMER: OK, then the *7:15* flight is all right.
AGENT: Is that one-way or round-trip?
CUSTOMER: Excuse me. I don't understand.
AGENT: *Do you* want to stay in *Manila* or *do you* want to come back here?
CUSTOMER: Oh, *I want* to stay in Manila.
AGENT: That's a one-way ticket. *$1,050.00*, please.
CUSTOMER: Here you are.
AGENT: Thank you very much. *Your ticket is for Flight #801* at *7:15 P.M.*
CUSTOMER: Thanks for your help.

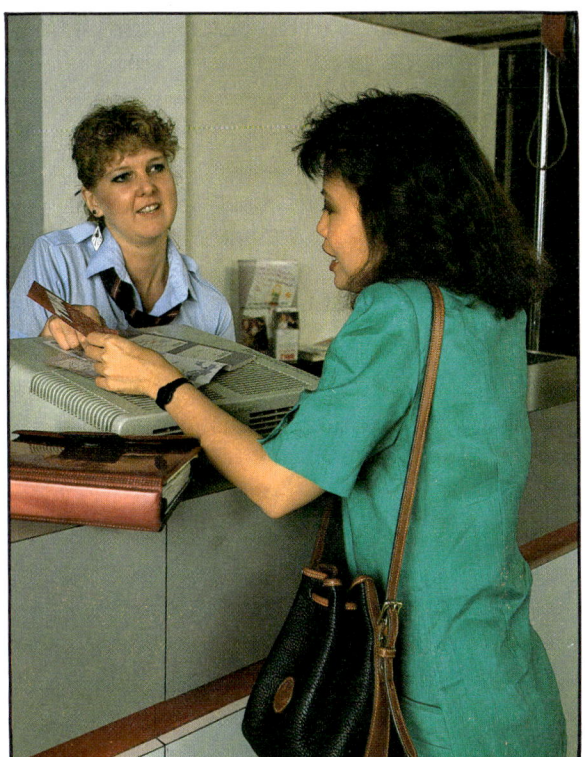

**Have similar conversations with a partner.**

1. Caracas/my parents
   October 3rd
   5:00 P.M./morning
   $317.00
   #217

2. Toronto/my sister
   April 5th
   7:55 A.M./evening
   $108.00
   #122

3. Jerusalem/my son
   January 1st
   6:45 P.M./afternoon
   $639.00
   #114

4. Tokyo/my grandparents
   June 21st
   10:50 A.M./evening
   $1,032.00
   #97

5. Bombay/my husband and me
   December 12th
   9:05 P.M./morning
   $984.00
   #66

6. London/my brother
   May 5th
   7:34 A.M./afternoon
   $403.00
   #100

## 4

**Work with a partner. Buy tickets for trips for you and your family. Use the conversation in Part 3.**

| GRAMMAR | | | | | | | | USEFUL LANGUAGE |
|---|---|---|---|---|---|---|---|---|
| I<br>They | want<br>'d like | to buy a ticket to Manila. | Do | you<br>they | want | to stay in Manila? | | How much is a one-way/round-trip ticket, please?<br>Excuse me.<br>I don't understand.<br>Thanks for your help. |
| She<br>He | wants<br>'d like | to arrive in New York by 3:30. | Does | she<br>he | | | | |
| What time<br>When | does | she<br>he | need<br>want | to leave here? | | | | |
| | do | they | | | | | | |

Unit 20  I don't feel well today.

# 1

**Listen to the names of the parts of the body.**

| | |
|---|---|
| teeth | arm |
| head | elbow |
| hair | hand |
| eye | finger |
| ear | chest |
| nose | stomach |
| mouth | leg |
| neck | knee |
| shoulder | foot |
| back | toe |

**Practice with a partner. Talk about these people. Make sentences like these:**

He has | *big ears.*
       | *a small nose.*

big
small
long
short

# 2

**Listen to the conversation and practice with a partner.**

A: *Mrs. Robbins* doesn't look very well.
   Does *she* feel all right?
B: No. *She* has a *bad headache.*
   *She* says it really hurts.

**Have similar conversations with a partner.**

1. Mr. Jones
   bad earache

2. Dr. Green
   bad toothache

3. Ms. Willis
   sore foot

4. Mr. Thompson
   sore knee

5. Ms. Avery
   bad backache

6. Mrs. Gonzales
   sore eye

7. Dr. Lee
   sore neck

8. Ms. Sutherland
   bad stomachache

# 3

**Listen to the conversation and practice with a partner.**

MAX: Hi! This is Max. Do you want to go to the beach today?
NED: *I'm* sorry. *I* don't feel well today.
MAX: Oh? What's the matter?
NED: *I* have *a bad cold.* I feel terrible.
MAX: That's too bad. Take care of *yourself,* OK?
NED: Thanks, Max.

NANCY: Well, does *Ned* want to go?
MAX: No, *he* doesn't feel well.
NANCY: Oh? What's the matter?
MAX: *He* has *a bad cold. He* feels terrible.
NANCY: That's too bad.

**Have similar conversations with partners.**

1. Cindy and Joe
   the measles

2. Jeff
   a fever

3. Nat
   a bad cough

4. Bonnie
   a sore throat

MAX: Nancy? Do *we* want to go to the beach?
NANCY: I don't know. Our friends are all sick. I feel lonely.
MAX: Me, too.
NANCY: Let's stay home.

| GRAMMAR | | | | | |
|---|---|---|---|---|---|
| I<br>They | have | the flu. | I<br>You<br>They | don't | feel well. |
| He<br>She | has | a bad headache. | He<br>She | doesn't | |

| USEFUL LANGUAGE |
|---|
| Does she feel all right?<br>It really hurts.<br>I feel terrible./lonely.<br>Take care of yourself. |

Unit 21   I usually get up at 7:30.

**1**

**Listen and practice with a partner.**

*I usually get up at 7:30,* but today is different.
Today *I'm getting up at 6:00.*

**Tell your partner about the pictures.**

1. Kate and Bob/have fruit for breakfast
   eggs

2. Carlos/take the subway to work
   the bus

3. We have soup for lunch
   sandwiches

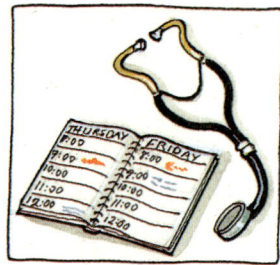

4. Mark go to the office
   doctor

5. Mrs. Kim make rice for dinner
   spaghetti

6. Vincent and I/do homework after dinner
   play baseball

7. I drink tea before bed
   milk

8. Nita go to bed at 10:30
   midnight

**2**

**Student A, ask Student B questions like this:**

A: How often do you *go to the movies on Saturday night?*
B: I *always go to the movies on Saturday night.*

**Now ask about these:**

eat dinner with your family, study after midnight, play tennis before lunch, get up before 6:00 A.M., take a bus to school, do your homework on a computer, eat lunch with a friend, and eat ice cream for breakfast.

**Students A and B, work with two other students who are partners, Students C and D. A, talk to C about B. B, talk to D about A.**

A (to C):  How often do you think _____ eats lunch with a friend ?
                               (Student B)
C: I think *he sometimes eats lunch with a friend.*
A: (If the answer is right): That's right.
   (If the answer is wrong): No, *he never eats lunch with a friend.*

**Student C, talk to A about D. Student D, talk to B about C.**

never

sometimes

often

always

## 3. Listen to the conversation and practice with a partner.

VIVIANA: Charles, you live in a cave in the Rocky Mountains. Please tell us about your life there.
CHARLES: Sure, Viviana. *I* usually *live* in *my* cave from October to May. It's a beautiful place, but people never come there.
VIVIANA: Never? *You* never *have* visitors?
CHARLES: Just the mice. But *I* always *see my* friends and family in the summer. *I'm* visiting *my* sister right now.
VIVIANA: So *your* life in the cave is always very quiet.
CHARLES: Well, it's usually quiet. But sometimes bad weather comes. Then the cave is exciting.
VIVIANA: *Do you* get bored?
CHARLES: Oh, no! *I'm* never bored. *I'm* always busy. Every day *I work* on *my* clothes and *my* boots. *I* always *exercise* and *I make* breakfast, lunch, and dinner.
VIVIANA: *Do you* have any fun?
CHARLES: Of course! *I'm* writing a book. That's fun.
VIVIANA: *You're* writing a book in your cave? How?
CHARLES: On my computer!

**Student A, you want to know about Charles and his life in a cave. Student B, you are Viviana. Start like this:**

A: Tell me about Charles and his life in a cave.
B: Sure. *He* usually *lives* in *his* cave from October to May. It's a beautiful place, but people never come there.
A: Never? *He* never *has* visitors?
B: _____

| GRAMMAR | | | | | | | USEFUL LANGUAGE |
|---|---|---|---|---|---|---|---|
| I | usually<br>never<br>sometimes<br>often<br>always | get up at 7:30. | Today | I | am | getting up<br>at 6:00. | I think . . .<br>Of course.<br>That's fun. |
| | | | | He<br>She | is | | |
| | | | | They | are | | |

Summary 4  Units 16–21

## 1
**Look at the picture. Then listen and write T (true), F (false), or I (I don't know).**

1. T
2. ___
3. ___
4. ___
5. ___
6. ___
7. ___
8. ___
9. ___
10. ___
11. ___
12. ___

## 2
**Listen and circle the letter of the best answer.**

a. Yes, there is.
b. Yes, it is.
c. Yes, I do.   *(c circled)*

1. a. Before 6:00 P.M. on Wednesday.
   b. I want to go round-trip.
   c. Yes, I like the train.

2. a. Yes, please. What kind of ice cream do you want?
   b. Yes, please. I'd like some vanilla ice cream.
   c. Yes, please. Today I'm getting up at 7:00.

3. a. I'm sorry. I don't have any tennis shoes.
   b. I'm sorry. I don't feel well.
   c. I'm sorry. I don't like the beach.

4. a. Yes, I am.
   b. Yes, it is.
   c. What kind of pie?

5. a. Yes, I have a lot of change.
   b. Yes, the bus is too expensive.
   c. Yes, I need some change.

6. a. No. She has a sore eye.
   b. No. She always takes the bus.
   c. No. He has a backache.

7. a. I'd like a sandwich.
   b. Never.
   c. I don't really want lunch.

8. a. They're $61.50.
   b. Thanks for your help.
   c. One-way or round-trip?

9. a. She says it really hurts.
   b. That's too bad. Please take care, OK?
   c. Do you feel OK?

10. a. No, I don't really like it.
    b. He likes it a lot.
    c. Me, too.

11. a. OK. I want to get a good seat.
    b. OK. It's 7:30 now.
    c. OK. I always get up before 7:00.

12. a. Oh, good. Let's relax.
    b. Yes, I really want one.
    c. No, I have some good ones.

Work with a partner for Parts 3 and 4. Student A, look at this page. Student B, look at the next page.

# STUDENT A

## 3

Listen to the conversation between Dennis Eubanks and his doctor.

Listen again. Write a "✓" for each question under the correct column. You have some answers. Listen for the other answers.

| How often does Dennis _____? | never | sometimes | often | always |
|---|---|---|---|---|
| • feel tired | | | | |
| • sleep seven hours (or more) at night | | | | |
| • have headaches | | | | |
| • have backaches | | | | |
| • eat pie or ice cream | | | | |
| • eat fruits and vegetables | | | | |
| • feel angry | | | | |
| • feel nervous | | | | |
| • swim | | | | |
| • run | | | | |

Check your answers with your partner. Start like this:

A: Dennis always feels tired, right?
B: That's right./No, he _____ feels tired.

## 4

Student A, start the conversation. Then listen to your partner and choose a good answer. Continue the conversation. Then try the conversation again. Choose different answers.

—Are you ready to order?

—Sure. There's no hurry.
—Today we have chicken or egg salad.

—I'm sorry. We don't have any spaghetti today.
—Yes, we do. Do you want a large or small soup?

—We have spinach salad and fruit salad today.
—OK. A large vegetable soup and some iced tea. Is that right?

# STUDENT B

## 3
**Listen to the conversation between Dennis Eubanks and his doctor.**

**Listen again. Write a "✓" for each question under the correct column. You have some answers. Listen for the other answers.**

| How often does Dennis _____? | never | sometimes | often | always |
|---|---|---|---|---|
| • feel tired <br> • sleep seven hours (or more) at night <br> • have headaches <br> • have backaches <br> • eat pie or ice cream <br> • eat fruits and vegetables <br> • feel angry <br> • feel nervous <br> • swim <br> • run | | | | |

**Check your answers with your partner. Start like this:**

A: Dennis always feels tired, right?
B: That's right./No, he _____ feels tired.

## 4
**Student B, listen to your partner and then choose a good answer. Continue the conversation. Then try the conversation again. Choose different answers.**

—Yes, please. What kind of sandwiches do you have?
—Hmm. Just a minute, please.

—Well, I don't really like chicken or egg salad. Do you have vegetable soup?
—Let's see . . . OK, I'm ready. I'd like some spaghetti, please.

—Oh, that's too bad. Well, what kind of salads do you have?
—Large, please. And some iced tea.

—I'd like the spinach salad, please.
—Yes, that's right.

## 5

You and your partner want to bake an apple pie. Student A has the list of things you need. Student B knows what's in the kitchen. A, look on the left. B, look on the right. Talk about the items and make a shopping list. Start like this:

A: We need some sugar. Do we have any?
B: No, we don't have sugar./Yes, we have some.
A: OK, let's write sugar on the list./OK.

**STUDENT A**    **STUDENT B**

SHOPPING LIST

_____

_____

_____

_____

## 6

Ask and answer questions like this with a partner. Write your partner's answers.

A: Do you like *classical music*?
B: Yes | a lot.
　　　| a little.

　No, not really.

| (name of partner) | Yes, a lot. | Yes, a little. | No, not really. |
|---|---|---|---|
| American movies | | | |
| the beach | | | |
| rainy days | | | |
| hot dogs | | | |
| iced cold drinks | | | |
| hot (spicy) food | | | |
| homework | | | |
| English | | | |

Tell about your partner to the class.

A: Kim likes classical music *a lot*.
　She *doesn't like* _____.

Unit 22   This restaurant was great last year.

## 1

**Listen to the conversation and practice with a partner.**

A: This *restaurant was great* last year.
B: I hope *it's* good now.

A: The *steaks were* tasty here last year.
B: I hope *they're* good now.

**Have similar conversations with a partner.**

1. music/nice    2. service/excellent    3. salads/wonderful    4. fish/fresh

5. chicken/delicious    6. vegetables/fresh    7. apple pie/fantastic    8. prices/reasonable

## 2

**Listen to the conversation and practice with a partner. Then have similar conversations using the pictures in Part 1.**

A: This *restaurant* is *terrible*.
B: I don't understand it. *It wasn't* bad last year.

A: The *steaks* are *awful*.
B: I don't understand it. *They weren't* bad last year.

## 3

**Tell your partner about a restaurant you know.**

A: I was at _____ last year.
         (Name of restaurant)
B: How was the *food*?
A: The *food* was *wonderful*.
B: How was the *service*?
A: The *service* _____.

Carol's RESTAURANT

To help us serve you better...

           Good    OK    Terrible

food _____
service _____
prices _____
_____
_____

## 4

**Listen to the conversation and practice with a partner.**

WAITER: Is everything OK, sir?
CUSTOMER: No, it isn't. These *spoons* are *dirty!*
WAITER: Oh, I'm very sorry. Here are some *clean spoons*, sir. I'm sorry the other ones were *dirty*.
CUSTOMER: That's all right. Thank you.
WAITER: Is everything else all right?
CUSTOMER: No, it isn't. This *chair* is *broken,* too.
WAITER: Oh, I'm sorry, sir. Here's a *good chair*, sir. I'm sorry the other one was *broken*.
CUSTOMER: That's all right. Thank you.

**Have similar conversations with a partner.**

1. noodles   napkins
   cold      dirty
   hot       clean

2. carrots   fork
   burned    bent
   fresh     new

3. glasses   knife
   cracked   dirty
   new       clean

4. rolls     cup
   stale     broken
   fresh     new

## 5

**Listen to the conversation and finish it with a partner. Use the pictures in Part 4.**

WAITER 1: What's wrong?
WAITER 2: Nothing. I'm just angry.
Those *spoons* weren't *dirty*—they were *clean*.
That *chair* wasn't *broken*—it was *good*.
Those *noodles* _____.
That man was crazy!

| GRAMMAR | | | | | | | USEFUL LANGUAGE |
|---|---|---|---|---|---|---|---|
| This restaurant | is | terrible | now. | | | | I hope . . . |
| | was / wasn't | | last year. | | | | How is/was the food? |
| | | | | | | | Is everything OK? |
| The steaks | are | awful | now. | These spoons are | dirty. | | That's all right. |
| | were / weren't | great | last year. | This chair is | broken. | | |

Unit 23    A week ago, we were in Florida. . .

## 1

**Listen to the conversations and practice with a partner.**

A: A *week* ago, we were in *Florida*, and it *rained* every day.
B: That's a shame. What did you do?
A: We *stayed inside*.

A: A *month* ago, we were in *San Diego*, and it was *warm* every day.
B: That's nice. What did you do?
A: We *went to the zoo*.

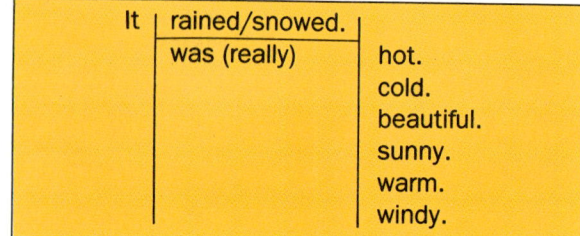

**Have similar conversations with a partner.**

1. year/Mexico
   really hot
   went swimming

2. few days/Boston
   really cold
   cooked a lot

3. while/Los Angeles
   beautiful
   took long walks

4. short time/London
   rained
   went to museums

**Practice with a partner.**

A: Where were you a *week* ago?
B: _____
A: What did you do?
B: _____

| It | rained/snowed. | |
|---|---|---|
|    | was (really)   | hot. |
|    |                | cold. |
|    |                | beautiful. |
|    |                | sunny. |
|    |                | warm. |
|    |                | windy. |

## 2

**Listen to the conversation and practice with a partner.**

A: What *was* the *high* temperature in *Atlanta yesterday*?
B: It *was 77* degrees.
A: What *'s* the *high* temperature there *today*?
B: *79*.

**Work with a partner. Student A, look at the chart on the left. Student B, look at the chart on the right. Ask and answer questions to finish your charts. Use the conversation.**

### STUDENT A

**The Weather in U.S. Cities***

| Cities | Yesterday High/Low | Today High/Low |
|---|---|---|
| Atlanta |  | 79/55 |
| Boston | 48/37 |  |
| Chicago | 72/57 |  |
| Houston |  | 84/57 |
| Los Angeles | 66/62 |  |
| Miami |  | 84/72 |
| New York |  | 66/52 |
| San Francisco | 63/55 |  |
| Washington, D.C. |  | 75/50 |

*Temperatures are in Fahrenheit.

### STUDENT B

| Cities | Yesterday High/Low | Today High/Low |
|---|---|---|
| Atlanta | 77/54 |  |
| Boston |  | 61/40 |
| Chicago |  | 74/56 |
| Houston | 83/52 |  |
| Los Angeles |  | 70/58 |
| Miami | 82/75 |  |
| New York | 61/53 |  |
| San Francisco |  | 65/50 |
| Washington, D.C. | 70/46 |  |

*Temperatures are in Fahrenheit.

## 3

**Listen to the conversation and practice with a partner.**

ANDY: Hi! How was your vacation?
BOB: It was OK.
ANDY: Where were you?
BOB: Well, on *Monday and Tuesday,* we were *at the beach.*
ANDY: Oh. Was it fun?
BOB: Not much. It was *cold and windy.*
ANDY: That's too bad. Where were you after that?

**Continue the conversation with a partner.**

1. Wednesday and Thursday
   in the mountains
   very rainy

2. Friday and Saturday
   in a large city
   very hot

BOB: On Sunday, we were in a perfect place.
ANDY: Oh. Was it fun?
BOB: Yes, it was warm and sunny.
ANDY: Where were you?
BOB: At home!

**Practice the conversation again. This time, Bob's sister tells about Bob's vacation. (Use "he.")**

| GRAMMAR | | | | | | USEFUL LANGUAGE |
|---|---|---|---|---|---|---|
| A week ago, | it | rained. | I | was | at the beach. | Where were you a week ago? |
| | | was hot. | He | | | What did you do? |
| | | | She | | | That's a shame. |
| | | | We | were | | That's nice. |
| | | | You | | | Was it fun? |
| | | | They | | | Not much. |

Unit 24  I called all day.

## 1

**Listen to the conversation and practice with a partner.**

MOTHER: Sarah, how are you? How's Annie?
BABYSITTER: Everything's fine. Why?
MOTHER: I called all day. You weren't home.
BABYSITTER: Oh, we were out.

MOTHER: I called you at 9:00.
BABYSITTER: Let's see. At 9:00, we walked to the park.

MOTHER: I called you at *10:30*.
BABYSITTER: From *10:00* to *11:00*, we *visited Bob*.

9:00/walk to the park

10:00–11:00/visit Bob

**Have similar conversations with a partner.**

1. 11:30
   11:00–12:00/watch TV at Bob's

2. 12:00
   12:00/stop at a restaurant for lunch

3. 1:00
   12:30–1:30/bake cookies with Bob

4. 1:35
   1:30–1:45/wait for the bus

5. 2:30
   2:00–3:00/play tennis

6. 3:10
   3:00–3:15/rest for a while

7. 3:25
   3:15–3:30/wait for the bus again

8. 4:15
   3:45–4:30/plant flowers in the yard

**Student A, you are the child's father. Student B, you are the child's mother. Have a phone conversation about your child's day.**

FATHER: What did Sarah and Annie do today?
MOTHER: Well, at *9:00* they *walked to the park*.
FATHER: Uh-huh. What did they do after that?
MOTHER: Well, from *10:00* to *11:00* they . . .

## 2

**Listen to the conversation and practice with a partner.**

MOTHER: Did you enjoy your day with Grandma?
RAY: Yes. It was great!
MOTHER: What did you do?
RAY: *I painted my bicycle.*
MOTHER: How was that?
RAY: OK. But there was one problem.
MOTHER: What happened?
RAY: *I spilled the paint in the closet.*
MOTHER: Oh, no! Did *you* spill it all?
RAY: Yes—it was a big mess! But don't worry. Grandma cleaned it up.
MOTHER: Poor Grandma! Did *you* help?
RAY: Yes, *I* did.
MOTHER: What else happened?
RAY: Well . . .

**Have similar conversations with a partner.**

1. Annie and I
   bake cookies
   the sugar
     on the table

2. Max
   water the plants
   the water
     on the rug

3. Max and I
   wash the dog
   the shampoo
     in the bathtub

4. Max and Annie
   feed the dog
   the dog food
     on the floor

## 3

**Student A, tell Student B about something that you or someone that you know spilled. Then change roles.**

A: Last *week*, *my brother* spilled the *salt* in the *kitchen.*
B: Did *he* clean it up?
A: Yes, *he* did./No, *my mother* cleaned it up.

| GRAMMAR | | | | USEFUL LANGUAGE |
|---|---|---|---|---|
| I called you at 9:00. | What | did | they | do? | From 10:00 to 11:00, . . . |
| | | They | walked to the park. | It was great! |
| | Did | they | enjoy their day? | How was that? |
| | | you | help? | What happened? |
| | | | | Don't worry. |

Unit 25  How was the party?

## 1

**Listen to the conversation and practice with a partner.**

FATHER: Hi! How was the party?
Did you *like it*?
ERIN: I *liked it*, but Cindy didn't.
She stayed in the corner all evening.

**Listen to the conversation and practice with a partner.**

FATHER: Did you *listen to music*?
ERIN: I *listened to music*, but Cindy didn't.
She stayed in the corner all evening.

**Have similar conversations with a partner.**

1. dance

2. play ping-pong

3. enjoy the food

4. talk to your friends

5. laugh a lot

6. help with the dishes

7. play the piano

8. watch TV

## 2

**Listen to the conversation between Erin's father and her friends, Carl and Jason. Continue the conversation. Use 1–8 from Part 1.**

FATHER: Was it a good party?  Did you *like it*?
CARL and
JASON: Erin *liked it*, but we didn't.
We watched TV all evening.
FATHER: Did you *listen to music*?
CARL and
JASON: _____

## 3

**Listen to the conversation between Erin and her friend, Adam. Adam didn't go to the party.**

ADAM: How was the party last night?
ERIN: I really *enjoyed* it. It *was* my kind of music, and I *danced* a lot.
ADAM: Did they serve any food?
ERIN: Yes. The food *was* great. I really *liked* the chicken dish.
ADAM: Who was there?
ERIN: Most of our friends *were* there.
ADAM: Did you stay late?
ERIN: I stayed until midnight. I *didn't want* to go home.

## 4

**Now Adam is talking to Cindy. Student A, you are Adam; Student B, you are Cindy. You didn't like the party at all. Student A, ask the questions from Part 3 to Student B.**

ADAM: How was the party last night?
CINDY: I really *didn't enjoy* it. It *wasn't* my kind of music, and I *didn't dance* at all.
ADAM: _____

## 5

**Work with a partner. Ask about a party. Use the conversations from Parts 3 and 4. Start like this:**

A: I went to a party last week.
B: Did you enjoy it?
A: I really *enjoyed/didn't enjoy* it.
B: Why?
A: _____

| GRAMMAR | | | | USEFUL LANGUAGE |
|---|---|---|---|---|
| Did you like it? | I really | liked | it. | How was the party? |
| I liked it, but Cindy didn't. | | didn't like | | Until midnight. |
| | | | | It was/wasn't my kind of music. |

Unit 26   When I was 17, I broke my arm.

## 1

**Listen to the conversations and practice with a partner.**

A: When I was *17*, I *broke my arm.*
B: Oh? How did you *break it*?
A: I *fell from a ladder.*
B: That's too bad.

A: When I was *20*, I got *my first job.*
B: Oh? How did you *get it*?
A: I *went to my father's company.*
B: That was lucky.

**Have similar conversations with a partner.**

1. 22/won tickets to Hawaii
   win them
   wrote a poem

2. 24/had an accident
   have it
   hit a fence with my bicycle

3. 25/met my husband
   meet him
   sold him my bicycle

4. 26/found a better job
   find it
   found it in the paper

**Listen to the conversation and practice with a partner.**

A: Now I'm 28. This year, I had a baby.
B: When did you have it?
A: Last month.
B: Congratulations!

## 2

**Here's what happened to Elizabeth:**

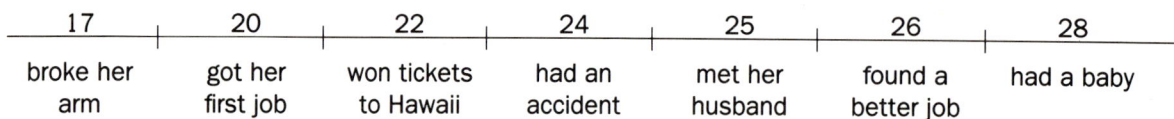

| 17 | 20 | 22 | 24 | 25 | 26 | 28 |
|---|---|---|---|---|---|---|
| broke her arm | got her first job | won tickets to Hawaii | had an accident | met her husband | found a better job | had a baby |

**Tell your partner about similar events in your life.**

68

## 3

**Listen to the conversation and practice with a partner.**

LISA: Hello?
TOM: Hello, Lisa?
LISA: Yes?
TOM: Hi, this is Tom. How was Sunday?
LISA: Not so good.
TOM: What happened?
LISA: Well, I wanted to see my *sister.* But I had lots of problems.
TOM: Oh? What happened?
LISA: Well, first I lost my *apartment keys.*
TOM: Did you find *them?*
LISA: Yes, under the sofa. Then I left, but I forgot my *glasses.*
TOM: Oh, no! Did you go back for *them?*
LISA: Yes, but when I went back, it began to rain. So I took the bus.
TOM: Well, how *was* your *sister?*
LISA: I don't know. I didn't see *her.*
TOM: Why not?
LISA: I took the wrong bus.

**Have similar conversations with a partner.**

1. parents
   pocketbook
   watch

2. brother
   brother's new address
   wallet

3. friend's concert
   concert ticket
   jacket

4. sister's new baby boy
   checkbook
   baby gift

**Student A, tell Student B the story of Lisa's problems on Sunday. Start like this:**

Lisa wanted to see her sister, but she had lots of problems. First, she lost her apartment keys. Then. . .

## 4

**Tell your partner about something you lost or forgot recently.**

A: Last *week*, I lost my *English book.*
B: Did you find *it?*
A: _____

| GRAMMAR | | | | USEFUL LANGUAGE |
|---|---|---|---|---|
| Did you How did you | find | them? | | That was lucky. Congratulations! |
| I | found | them | under the sofa. | |

Summary 5  Units 22–26

## 1

**Listen and circle the letter of the best answer.**

a. Oh, no! What happened?
b. Oh, no! Did he do it?
c. Oh, no! Is she OK?

1. a. No, he didn't.
   b. No, not much.
   c. No, it wasn't.

2. a. You're welcome.
   b. That's all right.
   c. Excuse me.

3. a. Was she OK?
   b. Good idea.
   c. How did you break it?

4. a. Did you find them?
   b. Did you lose them?
   c. Where did they lose them?

5. a. Is it expensive?
   b. That's nice.
   c. Oh, I'm very sorry.

6. a. They were excellent.
   b. It was great.
   c. The service was terrible.

7. a. Not much.
   b. They were really fun.
   c. It was really fun.

8. a. Yes, I am.
   b. Yes, I did.
   c. Yes, it was.

9. a. I hope it's good now.
   b. I hope it was good last week.
   c. I hope they're good now.

10. a. Oh, was it nervous?
    b. Oh, was it fun?
    c. Oh, was it a mess?

11. a. It's 78 degrees.
    b. There were 78 degrees.
    c. It was 78 degrees.

12. a. I stopped at Susan's apartment for dinner.
    b. I went home.
    c. That's a good idea.

## 2

**Look at the pictures. Listen to three sentences about each picture. Circle the letter of the best sentence.**

 1. a b c

 2. a b c

 3. a b c

 4. a b c

 5. a b c

 6. a b c

 7. a b c

 8. a b c

Work with a partner for Parts 3 and 4. Student A, look at this page. Student B, look at the next page.

# STUDENT A

## 3

**Listen to the phone conversations. Circle "good news" or "bad news." Then write any information that is missing.**

(good news)   bad news
Where: Under the bed.
When: _Five minutes ago._

1. good news   bad news
   Where: In the drugstore.
   When: _____

2. good news   bad news
   Where: _____
   When: On Saturday.

3. good news   bad news
   Where: _____
   When: Two days ago.

4. good news   bad news
   Where: In New York.
   When: _____

5. good news   bad news
   Where: On First Avenue across from the post office.
   When: _____

6. good news   bad news
   Where: _____
   When: Last Friday.

**Check your answers with your partner. Ask about your missing information.**

A: Was it good or bad news?
B: *Good news.*
   Where was it?
A: *Under the bed.*
   When did it happen?
B: *Five minutes ago.*

## 4

**Student A, start the conversation. Then listen to your partner and choose a good answer. Continue the conversation. Then try the conversation again. Choose different answers.**

—Did you have a good vacation?

—Where did you go in the U.S.?
—Terrible? Was it too hot?

—Oh, that's really too bad. Did you go to the beach?
—What was your favorite place?

—That's a shame.
—Were the people friendly in Florida?

# STUDENT B

## 3

**Listen to the phone conversations. Circle "good news" or "bad news." Then write any information that is missing.**

(good news)  bad news
Where: _Under the bed._
When: Five minutes ago.

1. good news   bad news
   Where: _____
   When: A week ago.

2. good news   bad news
   Where: On the beach.
   When: _____

3. good news   bad news
   Where: In the park.
   When: _____

4. good news   bad news
   Where: _____
   When: Last week. On Wednesday.

5. good news   bad news
   Where: _____
   When: At 6:30 last night.

6. good news   bad news
   Where: At Nix Electronics on Park St.
   When: _____

**Check your answers with your partner. Ask about your missing information.**

A: Was it good or bad news?
B: *Good news.*
   Where was it?
A: *Under the bed.*
   When did it happen?
B: *Five minutes ago.*

## 4

**Student B, listen to your partner and then choose a good answer. Continue the conversation. Then try the conversation again. Choose different answers.**

—Well, Bangkok was interesting, but the weather was terrible.
—Yes, it was wonderful.

—All over.
—Yes. It was 100 degrees every day. And our hotel didn't have an air conditioner.

—Florida. It's a large state in the south. It has lots of beaches, and it's warm and beautiful.
—Yes. Three times, but there were a lot of people there.

—Yes, I know. We're glad to be home.
—There weren't many people around, but the fish were friendly.

# 5

**Take a piece of paper. In ten minutes, make as many sentences as you can. Choose words from 1, 2, 3, 4, and 5.**

<u>Last Tuesday</u>¹, <u>the musician</u>² <u>played</u>³ <u>a violin</u>⁴ <u>at the concert</u>⁵.

<u>Yesterday</u>¹, <u>my sister</u>² <u>found</u>³ <u>the apartment keys</u>⁴ <u>in the refrigerator</u>⁵.

**WHEN?**
1. At _____ A.M./P.M.   Yesterday              In _____ (month)
   After class            A day/week/year ago
   Before bed             When I was            Last _____ (day of week)
                          _____ (age)

**WHO?**
2. the musician           my sister             you
   the teacher            my friend             _____ (name of student)
   the children           I

**DID WHAT?**
3. washed                 played                lost
   cleaned                bought                liked
   broke                  found

**WHAT?**
4. a jacket               a ball                a wallet
   the apples             some music            some ice cream
   a violin               the apartment keys    a camera
   some flowers           the bus

**WHERE?**
5. at a restaurant        at the concert        in the sink
   in the mountains       in Australia          in the refrigerator
   at the beach           in his/her pocket     under the table
   at an expensive store  in the kitchen

**Work in teams. A student from Team A says a sentence. It must be a good sentence in English. Then a student from Team B says a different sentence. Continue until one team can't make any more new sentences.**

Unit 27  Please, can you help me?

## 1

**Listen to the conversation and practice with a partner.**

A: *I lost my glasses* and *I* can't *see!* Please, can you help *me?*
B: Sure. I can help!

**Have similar conversations with a partner.**

1. My mother
   took my father's medicine
   walk very well

2. Kiki and Ken
   spent all their money at the zoo
   take the bus home

3. I
   hurt my back
   get up

4. My husband
   caught a big fish
   pull it in

5. We
   took a nap on the beach
   find our camera

6. My daughter
   put her finger in a bottle
   get it out

## 2

**Ask three other students in your class these questions:**

A: Can you *speak Italian?*
B: Yes, I can./No, I can't.

|  | (Student 1) | (Student 2) | (Student 3) |
|---|---|---|---|
| ...use a computer? |  |  |  |
| ...take good photos? |  |  |  |
| ...cook? |  |  |  |
| ...drive a car? |  |  |  |
| ...ride a horse? |  |  |  |
| ...play tennis? |  |  |  |

## 3

**Listen to the conversation and practice with a partner.**

CALLER: Hello. Can you send an ambulance to *First Street and Central Avenue?* Please hurry!

OPERATOR: Yes. I'm sending one right now. Now please tell me what happened. I can give the information to the people in the ambulance.

CALLER: *A plant fell out of a window and hit my girlfriend.* I think *it* broke *her arm.*

OPERATOR: Can *she move it?*

CALLER: No, *she* can't.

OPERATOR: OK. Please stay right there. The ambulance is coming.

**Have similar conversations with a partner.**

1. 19th St. and River Ave.
   A tricycle hit my grandmother.
   knee/walk

2. 11th St. and King Ave.
   A piece of ice fell on my son.
   back/get up

3. 12th St. and Bloom Ave.
   My brother hit my little sister.
   finger/move it

4. 27th St. and Sun Ave.
   A dog bit me.
   hand/move it

| GRAMMAR | | | | | | USEFUL LANGUAGE |
|---|---|---|---|---|---|---|
| She | can | | walk. | Can you help | me? | I can help. |
| | Can | she | walk? | | him? | Can you send an |
| | | | | | her? | ambulance? |
| Yes, | she | can. | | | us? | |
| No, | | can't. | | | them? | |

# Unit 28 How many do you need?

## 1

**Listen to the conversation and practice with a partner.**

DONNA: Let's go to the drugstore. I have to buy some *Band-Aids*.
GAIL: Oh, I have some. *How many* do you need?
DONNA: Just a *few*.
GAIL: Oh, you can use mine.
DONNA: Thanks! Now we can stay home!

**Have similar conversations with a partner. Use these count and noncount nouns. Use "how much" and "a little" with noncount nouns.**

| COUNT | |
|---|---|
| cotton balls | cold tablets |
| vitamins | safety pins |
| cough drops | |

| NONCOUNT | |
|---|---|
| foot powder | shampoo |
| bath oil | toothpaste |
| mouthwash | |

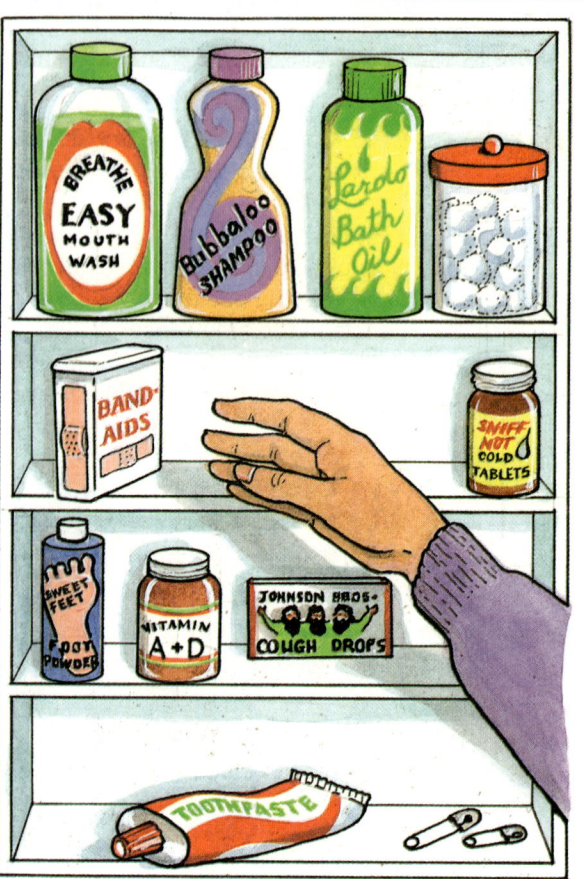

## 2

**Student A, look at the shopping list on the left. Ask Student B about the food you don't know about. Student B, look at the shopping list on the right, and ask Student A about the food you don't know about.**

A: How *much milk* do we have?
B: A lot.

B: How *many cookies* do we have?
A: A few.

### STUDENT A

| | none | a little/ a few | a lot |
|---|---|---|---|
| Milk | | | |
| Cookies | | ✓ | |
| Tea | | ✓ | |
| Oranges | | | |
| Ice Cream | | | |
| Eggs | ✓ | | |
| Crackers | | | |
| Sugar | | ✓ | |
| Apples | | | |
| Bread | | | |
| Tomatoes | | | ✓ |
| Butter | | ✓ | |

### STUDENT B

| | none | a little/ a few | a lot |
|---|---|---|---|
| Milk | | | ✓ |
| Cookies | | | |
| Tea | | | |
| Oranges | ✓ | | |
| Ice Cream | | ✓ | |
| Eggs | | | |
| Crackers | | | ✓ |
| Sugar | | | |
| Apples | | ✓ | |
| Bread | | | ✓ |
| Tomatoes | | | |
| Butter | | | |

## 3

**Listen to the conversation and practice with a partner.**

PHARMACIST: Hello. May I help you?
JUSTIN: Well, yes. I need some advice. I'm taking *Mason's Cough Drops* for a bad *cough*.
PHARMACIST: *Mason's*? Are you feeling better?
JUSTIN: Yes—I mean, no. My *cough* is better, but I can't stay awake at work.
PHARMACIST: *How many drops* do you take?
JUSTIN: I take *a few drops* every hour—just as it says right here.
PHARMACIST: No, no. It says, "Take *two cough drops* every four hours."
JUSTIN: Oh, I'm taking too *many cough drops*.
PHARMACIST: That's right.
JUSTIN: I'm glad I asked.
PHARMACIST: It's a good thing you did!

**Have similar conversations with a partner:**

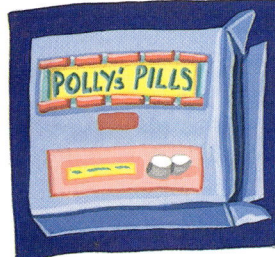 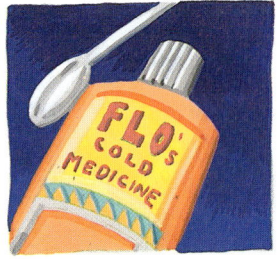  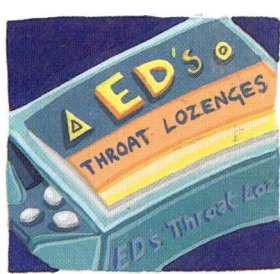

1. Polly's Pills
   backache
   pills
   two pills

2. Flo's Cold Medicine
   cold
   teaspoons
   two teaspoons

3. Sam's Syrup
   stomachache
   tablespoons
   one tablespoon

4. Ed's Throat Lozenges
   sore throat
   lozenges
   three lozenges

## 4

**Student A, you are the pharmacist. Student B, you are the customer. Use the conversation from Part 4. Talk about medicines you know.**

| GRAMMAR | USEFUL LANGUAGE |
|---|---|
| How \| many Band-Aids \| do you need? <br>       \| much powder \| <br><br> I'm taking too \| many cough drops. <br>                 \| much syrup. | A few. <br> A little. <br> A lot. <br> None. <br> I need some advice. <br> I'm glad I asked. |

# Unit 29  It's the nicest restaurant around.

## 1

**Listen to the conversation and practice with a partner.**

A: Which are *cheaper, apples* or *oranges?*
B: *Apples* are *cheaper* than *oranges.*
A: Which are *the cheapest?*
B: *Apples* are *the cheapest* fruits in the basket.
A: Which are *more expensive, pears* or *oranges?*
B: *Pears* are *more expensive* than *oranges.*
A: Which are *the most expensive?*
B: *Pears* are *the most expensive* fruits in the basket.

Add *-er* and *-est* after most short adjectives or adjectives that end with *-y*:
cheap → cheaper/cheapest
qui-et → quieter/quietest
happ-y → happier/happiest
Use *more* and *the most* before most long adjectives:
ex-pen-sive → more/the most expensive
in-tel-li-gent → more/the most intelligent

## 2

**Work with a partner. Talk about these people.**

A: Who's *the oldest?*
B: *Mr. King* is *the oldest.*
A: Who's *younger, Sam* or *Fanny?*
B: _____ is *younger.*
A: Who's *taller, John* or *Dick?*
B: *John* is *taller* than *Dick.*
A: Who's *shorter, Dick* or *Kate?*
B: _____ is *shorter.*

| NAME | AGE | NAME | HEIGHT |
|---|---|---|---|
| Mr. King | 75 | Rosa | 5' 4" |
| Mrs. King | 70 | John | 6' 3" |
| Sam King | 43 | Kate | 5' 1" |
| Fanny King | 42 | Dick | 5' 11" |
| Jane King | 16 | | |

## 3

**What's your opinion? Practice the conversation with a partner.**

A: In my opinion, *cars* are *more comfortable* than *buses.*
B: I agree./I don't agree. I think _____.
A: *Trains* are the *most comfortable* of all.
B: I agree./I don't agree.

**Have similar conversations with a partner. Use this information.**

| comfortable | bicycle | car | train | bus | plane |
|---|---|---|---|---|---|
| intelligent | monkey | horse | dog | fish | people |
| beautiful | jungle | city | desert | mountains | beach |

# 4

**Listen to the conversation and practice with a partner.**

A: Would you like to *have dinner* after work?
B: I'm sorry, I can't. I have to *meet a friend*.
A: Well, how about tomorrow?
B: Sure. I'd like that.
A: Great! Would you like to go to *The Paradise* or *John's Pizza*?
B: Well, *The Paradise* is *nicer* than *John's Pizza*.
A: That's true. It's the *nicest restaurant* around. Let's go there.

**Have similar conversations with a partner.**

1. play tennis
   study for a test
   the park/the tennis club
   cheap
   tennis court

2. go to the library
   go to work
   the University Library/ the City Library
   quiet
   library

3. see a movie
   visit my mother
   *The Woman in Black*/ *The Fast Tango*
   exciting
   movie

4. have coffee
   go to a meeting
   The Yellow Café/ Jo's Coffee Shop
   close
   coffee shop

5. go swimming
   take a test
   the college pool/ the club pool
   large
   pool

6. go to a museum
   clean my apartment
   the art museum/ the natural history museum
   interesting
   museum

7. hear some jazz
   go to the dentist
   Sweet Music/Little Ned's
   comfortable
   jazz spot

8. have lunch
   go to another class
   Sam's/The River Café
   fast
   lunch club

| GRAMMAR | | | | USEFUL LANGUAGE |
|---|---|---|---|---|
| Apples | are | cheaper | than oranges. | I'm sorry, I can't. |
| | | the cheapest | of all. | I have to meet a friend. |
| Mr. King | is | older | than Mrs. King. | How about tomorrow? |
| | | the oldest | of all. | That's true. |
| Which | are | cheaper, | apples or oranges? | Let's go there. |
| | is | the cheapest? | | I agree./I don't agree. |
| Would you | like | to have dinner? | | |
| I'd | | that. | | |

Unit 30  I'm going to need your help.

## 1

**Listen to the conversation and practice with a partner.**

MR. HERBERT: Today we're going to plan the meeting to talk about the new computer. The meeting is going to be next Thursday, November 3rd, and I'm going to need your help.
MR. HERBERT: *First*, we're going to need *a report about other new computers.* Who can *write it?*
LENNY: Beth and I can *write it.*

**Have similar conversations with a partner.**

1. Second
   a room for the meeting
   reserve
   Beth: my secretary

2. Third
   help from Josh Todd and Ann and Jack Lake
   call
   Jean: I

3. Fourth
   help from Peter Kato of Art Associates
   contact
   Jean: I

4. Fifth
   help from Nancy Smith at CRP, Inc.
   call
   Jean: I

5. Next
   lunch from 12 to 1
   arrange
   Lenny: my assistant

6. Finally
   help from Dr. Cynthia Rose at Comptech, Inc.
   contact
   Jean: I

## 2

**Student A, you are Mr. Herbert. Complete Mr. Herbert's sentence. Use 1–6 from Part 1. Student B, you are Lenny.**

MR. HERBERT: Now, let's see. Lenny and Beth are going to write a report about other new computers.
LENNY: That's right.
MR. HERBERT: Beth's secretary _____ _____.

## 3

**Listen to the conversation and practice with a partner.**

JOSH: *Todd Advertising.* Good morning.
JEAN: *Mr. Josh Todd*, please.
JOSH: This is *Josh Todd*.
JEAN: This is Jean Beckman from Ace Electronics.
JOSH: Oh, yes. Hello, Ms. Beckman.
JEAN: We're going to have a meeting next Thursday, November 3rd. Can you come?
JOSH: No, I'm afraid I can't. I'm going to *attend a conference in London all week.*
JEAN: It's too bad you're going to miss it. It's going to be an interesting meeting.
JOSH: Well, let's talk in a few weeks.
JEAN: OK. Good-bye.
JOSH: Good-bye.

**Student A, you are Jean Beckman. Call other people about the meeting. Student B, answer the phone.**

1. Lake Advertising
   Ann or Jack Lake
   give a presentation
   on the 3rd

2. CRP, Inc.
   Ms. Nancy Smith
   be on vacation

3. Art Associates
   Mr. Peter Kato
   go to Washington
   that day

4. Comptech, Inc.
   Dr. Cynthia Rose
   meet with our
   president

## 4

**Student A, you are Jean. Tell Mr. Herbert (Student B) about your phone calls from Part 3. Start like this:**

JEAN: First, I called *Todd Advertising. Josh Todd* can't come to the meeting because *he's* going to *attend a conference in London all week.*
MR. HERBERT: Hmm. Sorry to hear that.
JEAN: Then I called *Lake Advertising. Ann and Jack Lake...*

| GRAMMAR | | | | USEFUL LANGUAGE |
|---|---|---|---|---|
| I | 'm | going to | need your help. plan the meeting. | Good morning. I'm afraid I can't. I'm sorry to hear that. Good-bye! |
| We | 're | | | |

# Summary 6  Units 27–30

## 1

**Listen and circle the letter of the best answer.**

a. Sure. She can.
(b.) Sure. I can.
c. Sure. She is.

1. a. Just a little, please.
   b. Just one, please.
   c. Just a few, please.

2. a. Paris is the most beautiful.
   b. Paris is beautiful.
   c. Paris is more beautiful than London.

3. a. No, she's going to study art.
   b. No, she doesn't. She studies art.
   c. No, she didn't. She studied art.

4. a. I'm coming!
   b. Can they ski?
   c. I'm going to come in a few hours.

5. a. That's better.
   b. That's too little.
   c. That's too many.

6. a. I know. It's the most expensive restaurant around.
   b. I know. I want to eat there tomorrow.
   c. I know. The prices are very good.

7. a. Yes, he can.
   b. Yes, I can.
   c. Yes, they did.

8. a. The ambulance is leaving right away.
   b. A doctor is in the ambulance.
   c. The ambulance is new.

9. a. I do.
   b. I am.
   c. I did.

10. a. I'm sorry. I have to visit my grandfather in the hospital.
    b. I'm sorry. She went to the beach yesterday.
    c. I'm sorry. I studied in the library last night.

11. a. I'm sorry. I can't.
    b. I don't agree.
    c. I'd like that.

12. a. I think so.
    b. I'm sorry to hear that.
    c. Please hurry.

## 2

**Listen to the sentences. In each sentence you will hear "can" or "can't." Circle the word you hear.**

(can)   can't

1. can   can't     2. can   can't
3. can   can't     4. can   can't
5. can   can't     6. can   can't
7. can   can't     8. can   can't
9. can   can't    10. can   can't

Work with a partner for Parts 3 and 4. Student A, look at this page. Student B, look at the next page.

# STUDENT A

## 3

Yesterday, Mr. and Mrs. Nash went away for the night. Their son, Rob, and two of his friends were home. Today, when Rob's parents came home, a lot of food was missing. Look at the picture. This is the Nash's refrigerator today. Your partner can see the Nash's refrigerator as it was yesterday. Ask and answer questions with your partner. Write the answers. Use the words in the box under the picture. Start like this:

A: How much *milk* was there yesterday?
B: *A lot.* How much is there today?
A: *A little.*

A: How many *hot dogs* were there yesterday?
B: *Twenty-four.* How many are there today?
A: *Seven.*

|  | Yesterday | Today |
|---|---|---|
| juice | _____ | _____ |
| hot dogs | _____ | _____ |
| cake | _____ | _____ |
| fish | _____ | _____ |
| eggs | _____ | _____ |
| carrots | _____ | _____ |
| ice cream | _____ | _____ |
| tomatoes | _____ | _____ |
| apples | _____ | _____ |
| milk | _____ | _____ |

**Work with a partner. Ask and answer questions like these:**

A: How *much milk* did Rob and his friends *drink*?
B: *A lot.* How *many hot dogs* did they *eat*?
A: *Seventeen.*

> a little   a lot   a few   _____
>                           (number)
> There's no _____.   There are no _____.

## 4

Student A, start the conversation. Then listen to your partner and choose a good answer. Continue the conversation. Then try the conversation again. Choose different answers.

—How are you?

—Oh, yes. The big test.
—Just four or five weeks? You're lucky. You had a bad accident.

—Why not? Homework's no problem.
—Listen, I have an idea. I can help you to move.

—You're going to learn to write with your left hand. I can teach you.
—Well, next December I'm going to move. You can help me then.

# STUDENT B

## 3

Yesterday, Mr. and Mrs. Nash went away for the night. Their son, Rob, and two of his friends were home. Today, when Rob's parents came home, a lot of food was missing. Look at the picture. This is the Nash's refrigerator as it was yesterday. Your partner can see the Nash's refrigerator today. Ask and answer questions with your partner. Write the answers. Use the words in the box under the picture. Start like this:

A: How much *milk* was there yesterday?
B: *A lot.* How much is there today?
A: *A little.*

A: How many *hot dogs* were there yesterday?
B: *Twenty-four.* How many are there today?
A: *Seven.*

|  | Yesterday | Today |
|---|---|---|
| juice | | |
| hot dogs | | |
| cake | | |
| fish | | |
| eggs | | |
| carrots | | |
| ice cream | | |
| tomatoes | | |
| apples | | |
| milk | | |

**Work with a partner. Ask and answer questions like these:**

A: How *much milk* did Rob and his friends *drink*?
B: *A lot.* How *many hot dogs* did they *eat*?
A: *Seventeen.*

```
a little   a lot   a few     _____
                             (number)
There's no _____.  There are no _____.
```

## 4

**Student B, listen to your partner and then choose a good answer. Continue the conversation. Then try the conversation again. Choose different answers.**

—Fine. My hand is doing well, but I can't use it for four or five weeks.
—Not so good. I'm going to move to a new apartment next Friday, and there's a big test next Saturday.

—Yes, but I can't do my homework.
—I can't move and study at the same time.

—No, no! It's too much for you. You're very busy.
—But I can't write.

—That's very nice. Thank you.

# 5

**Work in two teams. Take a piece of paper and write sentences like these about one of the cities on the chart. Do not write the name of the city.**

This city is *larger* than *Istanbul*, but *smaller* than *Hong Kong*.

(or)

This is the *coldest* city on the chart.

| Use these words: | | | |
|---|---|---|---|
| hot | cool | large | wet |
| warm | cold | small | dry |

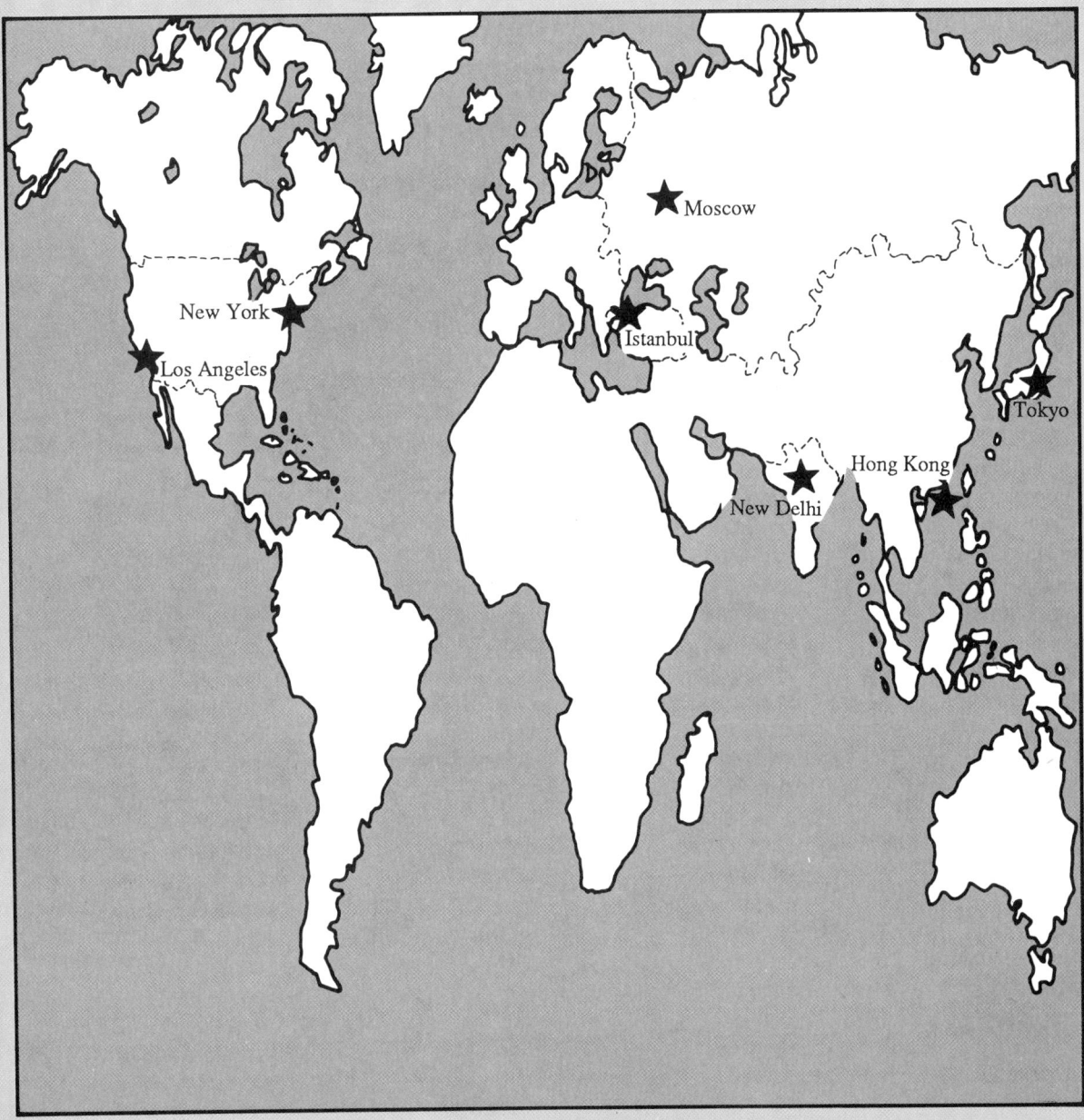

**The teams take turns. A student on Team A reads a sentence. Students on Team B listen and try to find the city on their charts. If a Team B student guesses the city in five seconds, Team B gets two points. If not, Team A gets a point.**

# Word and Phrase List

This word and phrase list contains the words and phrases found in *On Course 1*, Student Book. The list may not contain all of the words used in the accompanying cassette. The number next to each word indicates what unit it occurs in for the first time.

**A**
a *1*
a few *28*
a little *8*
a lot *12*
a quarter after *5*
about *4*
accident *26*
accountant *4*
across from *12*
add *29*
address *3*
adjective *29*
advertising *30*
advice *28*
afraid *30*
after *2*
afternoon *19*
again *2*
age *26*
ago *23*
agree *29*
air conditioner *10*
alarm clock *10*
always *21*
A.M. *5*
ambulance *27*
an *4*
and *1*
And you? *2*
angry *22*
another *16*
answer *2*
answering machine *S1*
anything *19*
apartment *10*
apple *16*
are *5*
Are you kidding? *13*
area *12*
aren't (are not) *7*
arm *20*
around *29*
arrange *30*
arrive *19*
art *30*
artist *4*
ask *2*
assistant *30*
associate *30*

at *2*
at all *25*
at home *23*
attend *30*
attractive *6*
aunt *1*
Australia *S5*
avenue *3*
awake *28*

**B**
baby *26*
back *20*
backache *20*
bad *20*
bake *24*
bakery *12*
ball *15*
ball game *17*
ballet *17*
balloon *13*
Band-Aid *28*
Bangkok *S5*
bank *12*
baseball *17*
basement *13*
basket *29*
basketball *7*
bath oil *28*
bathing suit *11*
bathrobe *11*
bathroom *9*
bathtub *9*
be on vacation *30*
beach *10*
beautiful *6*
because *14*
bed *9*
bedroom *9*
before *2*
begin *4*
behind *9*
bent *22*
best *14*
better *26*
between *12*
beverage *18*
big *10*
bike (bicycle) *7*
bill *16*

birthday *6*
black *6*
blanket *10*
block *12*
blond *5*
blouse *11*
blue *6*
blueberry *18*
body *20*
Bombay *19*
book *2*
bookstore *12*
bored *8*
Boston *1*
both *15*
bottle *27*
box *28*
boy *26*
boyfriend *6*
Brazil *4*
break *26*
breakfast *18*
broken *22*
broom *9*
brother *1*
brother-in-law *19*
brown *6*
bug *10*
burn *22*
bus *21*
businessman *4*
businesswoman *4*
busy *8*
but *6*
butter *28*
buy *6*
by *13*
By the way. . . *11*
bye *7*

**C**
cafe *29*
cake *18*
calculator *7*
call *24*
camera *15*
can/can't *30*
Canada *4*
car *7*
Caracas *19*

carrot *18*
cat *7*
catch *27*
cave *21*
cent *11*
chair *9*
change (n) *16*
change (v) *16*
chart *23*
cheap *11*
check *3*
checkbook *26*
chest *20*
Chicago *1*
chicken soup *13*
child (children) *13*
China *4*
chocolate *18*
choose *1*
circle *S2*
city *23*
class *1*
classical music *17*
clean *24*
clock *S1*
close (adj) *29*
closet *10*
clothes *6*
clue *S2*
coffee *18*
coffee shop *10*
cola *11*
cold (n) *20*
cold *8*
cold drink *8*
cold tablet *28*
college *14*
color *6*
come *27*
come in *7*
comedy *5*
comfortable *6*
company *3*
computer *7*
conference *30*
congratulations *26*
contact *30*
contest *S3*
continue *16*
conversation *1*

86

cook 4
cookie 24
cool S5
corner 25
cotton ball 28
cough 20
cough drop 28
count 28
country S1
court 29
cracked 22
cracker 28
crazy 22
cup 22
customer 18

**D**

dance 25
dark 4
dates 19
daughter 1
day 5
degrees 23
delicious 22
Denver 1
desert 29
desk 9
different 21
dining room 13
dinner 18
direction 12
directions S3
dirty 22
dish 25
divorced 4
do 13
do/did 23
doctor 4
does 2
dog 9
doll S2
dollar 11
don't (do not) 2
Don't worry. 24
dormitory 14
down 2
draw 9
dress 6
dresser 9
drink 11
driver 4
driveway 13
drugstore 12
dry cleaner 12

**E**

ear 20
early 5

eat 13
egg 21
eight 3
elbow 20
electronics 30
end 29
engineer 4
English 4
enjoy 13
equipment 16
evening 19
event 26
everything 22
exactly 5
example 3
excellent 10
exciting 21
exercise 21
exhibit 17
expensive 6
extra 6
Excuse me. 19
eye 20

**F**

factory 4
Fahrenheit 23
fall 26
false S4
family 1
family member 6
famous 5
fantastic 22
father 1
feed 24
feel 20
feet 13
fence 26
fever 20
few 28
finally 30
find 26
fine 2
finger 12
finish (v) 14
first 1
fish 7
flight 19
floor 24
Florida 16
flour S4
flower 24
flu 20
fly 13
follow 12
food 18
foot 20
foot powder 28

football 17
for 2
forget 26
fork 22
forty-five (time) 5
fountain 13
four 2
France 4
french fries 17
fresh 22
friend 4
from 1
front S1
fruit salad 18
full-time 14
fun 21

**G**

game 2
garden 7
gas station 12
Germany 4
get 26
get up 21
gift 6
girlfriend 6
give 27
glad 28
glasses (drinking) 10
glasses (eye) 7
glove (gloves) 6
go 5
go away S6
going well 14
good 22
Good idea. 8
good-looking 6
good-bye 14
Good luck! 14
Good morning. 30
grammar 1
grandfather 1
grandmother
  (grandma) 6
grandparents 13
grape 16
gray 6
great 13
Greece 4
green 6
grocery store 12
guitar 7

**H**

hair 4
half past 5
hall 10
hamburger 17

hand 20
hanger 10
happening 13
happy 8
hat 7
have 1
have lunch 8
Hawaii 26
he 1
head 20
headache 20
headphone 6
hear 26
heavy 5
height 29
helicopter 13
help 6
her 3
here 3
hers 15
hi 2
high 23
his 3
hit 26
hmm 6
hole 10
home 8
homework 21
Hong Kong S1
hope 22
horse 27
hospital 12
hot 8
hot dog 11
hot water 10
hotel 10
hour 5
house 10
how 21
How about . . . ? 29
How many . . . ? 28
How much . . . ? 6
How often . . . ? 21
hungry 8
hurry 7
hurt 20
husband 26

**I**

. . . I think. 4
I'd like (would like) 18
I'm (I am) 2
I'm afraid I can't. 30
I'm just fine. 8
I'm sorry, I can't. 29
ice 27
ice cream cone 11

87

ice machine 10
iced coffee 18
iced tea 18
in 5
in bad shape 7
information 27
inside 23
intelligent 29
interesting 30
international S3
introduce 1
is 1
isn't (is not) 10
Istanbul S6
it 1
Italian 27
Italy 4
item 6

## J
Japan 4
jazz 17
jazz club 29
Jerusalem 19
juice 16
jungle 29
just 21
just a minute 7

## K
key 7
kid (n) 9
kidding 13
kitchen 9
knee 20
knife 22
Korea 4

## L
ladder 26
lake 13
lamp 9
language 1
large 6
late 5
laundry bag 10
lawyer 4
leave 19
left (leave) 26
left (n) 9
leg 20
lemon S4
lemonade 18
lesson 16
let's (let us) 8
Let's see. . . . 11
letter 2
library 12

life 21
light 10
like 2
listen 1
little 28
live (v) 14
living room 9
London 14
lonely 20
long 23
long time 23
look 2
Los Angeles 1
lose 26
love 17
lovely 6
low 23
lozenge 28
lucky 26
lunch 18

## M
magazine 9
mail box 10
make 8
man 4
Manila 19
map 12
married 4
may 6
me 2
mean 2
measles 20
medicine 27
medium 6
meet 1
meeting 29
menu 11
mess 24
message S1
Mexico 23
Miami 1
middle 12
midnight 21
milk 18
mine 15
mirror 9
missing 19
modern art 17
money 14
monkey 29
month 19
more 29
morning 8
Moscow S6
most 25
mother 1
motorcycle 7

mouse 10
mouth 20
mouth wash 28
move 27
movie 8
Mr. 30
Ms. 30
much 3
museum 23
music 5
my 1
myself 19

## N
name 3
nap 27
napkin 22
nearby 10
neck 20
necklace 6
need 16
neighbor 4
neighborhood 12
nervous 8
never 21
new 25
New Delhi S6
New Mexico S1
New York 1
newspaper 9
next to 9
nice 1
no 2
noncount 28
noodle 22
noon 19
nose 20
not much 23
not so good 8
nothing 22
now 2
now and then 17
number 2
nurse 4

## O
o'clock 5
object 9
occupation S1
of 5
of course 21
office 21
oh 4
Oh, I'm sorry. 7
Oh, no. 5
OK 2
old 1

on 2
on time 5
one-way 19
onion 18
only 5
open 2
opera 17
opinion 29
or 4
orange 6
orange juice 18
order (v) 18
other 1
our 15
ours 15
out 24
over 3
over there 11

## P
page 2
paint 13
painting (n) 7
pants 6
parent 7
park (n) 13
park (v) 12
parking spot 17
part 16
partner 1
party 25
pear 29
pen 15
people 1
perfect 23
perfume 6
pharmacist 28
Philadelphia 19
phone (telephone) 3
photo 27
piano 7
picture 2
pie 18
piece 12
pillow 10
ping pong 25
pink 6
pitcher 15
place 12
plain 18
plan 30
plane 29
plant 24
play 2
please 2
P.M. 5
pocket S5
pocketbook 6

poem *26*
poor *24*
popular *6*
population *S6*
porch *13*
post office *12*
practice *1*
presentation *30*
president *30*
pretty much *17*
pretzel *11*
price *11*
problem *10*
program *5*
Puerto Rico *1*
pull *27*
purple *6*
purse *16*
put *27*

## Q
question *2*
quiet *29*
quietly *5*

## R
racket *16*
rain *23*
raincoat *6*
rainfall *S6*
rain hat *S3*
read *11*
ready *17*
reasonable *6*
recently *26*
record (n) *7*
red *6*
refrigerator *9*
relative *4*
relax *16*
remember *5*
repeat *2*
report *30*
reporter *13*
reserve *30*
rest *24*
restaurant *10*
rice *21*
ride *27*
right (n) *9*
right (affirmative) *2*
Right away. *3*
Right now. *14*
rock and roll *17*
Rocky Mountains *21*
rolls *22*
room *9*

round-trip *19*
rug *7*
run *13*
running shoes *11*
Russia *4*

## S
safety pin *28*
salad *18*
sale *S3*
salt *24*
San Diego *23*
San Francisco *1*
sandwich *17*
Santa Fe *S1*
save *14*
say *2*
scarf (scarves) *6*
schedule *19*
school *7*
seat *17*
second *1*
secret *S1*
secretary *4*
see *2*
sell *26*
semester *14*
send *3*
sentence *6*
serve *25*
service *22*
set *10*
shame *23*
shampoo *24*
she *1*
sheet *10*
shirt *6*
shoe *6*
shopping list *28*
short *1*
shortening *S4*
shoulder *20*
sick *8*
similar *1*
single *4*
sink *9*
sir *22*
sister *1*
sit *2*
size *11*
ski *7*
sleepy *8*
slipper *6*
small *6*
soap *10*
soccer *17*
socks *11*
sofa *9*

soft (softly) *4*
some *10*
someone *24*
something *24*
sometimes *21*
son *1*
sorry *7*
spaghetti *21*
Spain *4*
speak (spoken) *4*
spell *3*
spend *14*
spicy *S4*
spill *24*
spinach *18*
spoon *22*
sports *5*
spot *29*
spring (n) *13*
stale *22*
start *5*
stay *19*
steak *22*
stereo *7*
stomach *20*
stomachache *20*
stop *24*
stop at *S5*
stove *9*
strawberry *18*
street *3*
student *1*
study *13*
subway *21*
sugar *24*
suit *11*
summer *14*
sumo wrestling *S3*
sunglasses *6*
sunny *23*
sunscreen *16*
supermarket *14*
sure *5*
sweater *6*
swim *23*
swimming pool *10*

## T
table *9*
tablespoon *28*
take a break *8*
talk *6*
tall *1*
tango *S3*
tape *2*
tape recorder *7*
tasty *22*
taxi *3*

taxi driver *51*
tea *18*
teacher *2*
team *S2*
teaspoon *28*
teeth *20*
tell *2*
temperature *23*
tennis *16*
tennis shoes *16*
terrible *20*
test *8*
thank you *2*
that *1*
the *1*
the Philippines *4*
the United States *4*
theater *12*
their *14*
them *7*
then *5*
there *3*
these *1*
they *22*
they're (they are) *6*
thing *16*
think *4*
thirsty *8*
thirty (time) *5*
this *1*
three *3*
throat *20*
ticket *19*
tie *S3*
time *2*
tired *8*
to *1*
too many *28*
today *5*
toe *20*
together *17*
toilet *9*
Tokyo *19*
tomato *16*
tomorrow *7*
too *1*
toothache *20*
toothpaste *28*
Toronto *19*
tournament *17*
towel *10*
train *29*
tree *13*
tricycle *27*
true *S4*
try *11*
turn *12*
TV *5*

## U

umbrella 9
uncle 15
under 9
understand 19
until 25
use 4
useful 1
usually 21

## V

vacation 23
vanilla 18
vegetable 18
vending machine 16
very 1
Vietnam 4
view 10
violin S5
visit 14
visitor 21
vitamin 28

## W

wait 5
waiter 4
waitress 4
walk 23
wall 10
wallet 15
warm 6
was 22
wash 24
Washington, D.C. 19
wasn't 22
watch (n) 6
watch (v) 13
watch TV 24
wave (v) 13
we 8
weather 23
week 5
well 6
went/go 23
were 22
weren't 22
what 2
What kind of . . . ? 18
What's the matter? 8
when 5
where 9
while 23
white 6
who 1
whose 15
why 14
wife 1
win 26
window 15
windy 23
with 1
woman 4
wonderful 10
word 4
work 4
worker 4
wrestling 17
write 2
wrong 10
Wyoming S5

## Y

yard 24
year 19
yellow 6
yes 1
yogurt 18
yourself 20
you 1
young 1
your 2
You're welcome. 3
yours 15

## Z

zoo 23